St. Augustine's College,
Canterbury.

with every good wish
for the author.

by E. Lorna Kendall

A CITY NOT FORSAKEN

IF ANY MAN BUILD

A LIVING SACRIFICE (S.C.M. Press)

Watchmen Upon Thy Walls

STUDIES OF EUROPEAN MASTERS
OF THE SPIRITUAL LIFE

BY

E. LORNA KENDALL
M.A., PH.D.

E. Lorna Kendall.

FOREWORD BY THE BISHOP OF WAKEFIELD

THE FAITH PRESS
7 TUFTON STREET LONDON S.W. 1

FIRST PUBLISHED IN 1963

© *E. Lorna Kendall 1963*

PRINTED IN GREAT BRITAIN
in 10 point Garamond type
BY THE FAITH PRESS LTD
LEIGHTON BUZZARD

*For Geoffrey and Elizabeth
Lampe
with affection and gratitude*

FOREWORD

As the universe around us is made to disclose more and more of its secrets, and as the human power over natural processes becomes greater and greater, so the evidence for the supernatural life, the Divine Milieu, tested by first-hand experience, becomes more and more significant. Dr. Lorna Kendall has assembled from the lives and writings of European masters of the spiritual life enough evidence to encourage any one who looks for a 'city which hath foundations' to go to them for instruction. I find, after reading these studies, that I want, on the one hand, to go back to the original masterpieces in order to be better grounded in the classics, and, on the other hand, I want to look much more closely at what a contemporary such as Père Teilhard de Chardin is saying within our present situation. This may very well be Dr. Kendall's intention for all her readers.

There is a danger that the message of these mystics might fall on deaf ears, not because St. Benedict, Ramon Lull, and the rest all lived in the pre-atomic age, but because Christian experience has been so often described as though it could be independent of the baptismal experience. As a result a great many people to-day do not realize that they have been incorporated by their baptism into exactly the same life as the mystics are writing about. That life is not just what goes on inside an individual saint, as though he or she were the originator of it. That life is first of all Christ living his own risen and ascended life in one of the members of his mystical body. Into that life the humblest he or she who has been baptized has been incorporated. The initiative in the converse of the Lover with the Beloved lies with the unseen Lord, one and the same as the Son of Man who lived and died and was raised again in Palestine.

For so long now our English inheritance has conditioned us to think in terms of some kind of spiritual life which is to prepare us for the life which begins only after death and is fully realized only after the Last Judgment. It is only in recent years that the eschatology of the New Testament has been seriously re-examined, with the result that it has begun to be recognized that in the Person of Christ himself the post-Judgment state has been attained. In him, incarnate, crucified, risen, man is washed, justified, sanctified, to use the Pauline terms. To be baptized therefore is already, this side of the grave, to be taken into and united with that life-beyond-the-Judgment which the Risen Christ himself lives. That life which was hoped for in the end is therefore anticipated in this mortal life. The life in grace is a foretaste of the life in glory.

The people described in this book were all interesting characters no doubt, but their experience is no more and no less than their awakening to their baptismal state, and their response to that life which was not theirs by nature, but is his and became theirs by grace. Behind all that they describe is the ordinary process by which the ordinary Christian develops, the process of repeated restoration to the baptismal innocency through penitence and absolution, of daily prayer, and of regular participation in the Eucharist, and by taking with full seriousness the words of our Lord to his disciples, in other words by letting Heaven penetrate and mould their lives through the ordinary means of grace. Though they write from within a European life which no longer exists, they speak to that present life which exists in Christ anywhere at any time. That is the exciting thing about them.

✝ JOHN WAKEFIELD

May 1962

AUTHOR'S ACKNOWLEDGMENTS
AND NOTE

IT would be impossible to mention by name all whose help and encouragement have contributed to the making of this book. I should wish to record my especial gratitude to the Bishop of Wakefield for writing the Foreword; to the Rt. Revd. Monsignor R. J. Foster, Rector of Oscott College, Sutton Coldfield, for the generous loan of books; to my Extra-Mural students 1961–2, with whom the substance of this book was originally discussed; and to the staff of the Extra-Mural department of the University of Birmingham, of the Birmingham Library, and of the Faith Press for much patient, courteous and efficient help.

In the studies which follow, a considerable number of quotations from the writings of the authors concerned have been given, so that readers may feel they have an acquaintance, however slight, with the subject-matter under discussion; and in the hope that they will be impelled to read the complete books for themselves.

Christ Church College
    Canterbury

Feast of St. Barnabas, 1962

CONTENTS

CHAPTER 1

SAINT BENEDICT

c. 480–550

WHEN Jesus Christ was born in Bethlehem in the days of Herod the Great the response of the shepherds to the message of the angel was to say : 'Let us now go even unto Bethlehem, and see this thing which is come to pass, which the Lord hath made known unto us.' [1] The truth of the Christian Gospel has ever been startling in its very simplicity, and amongst the simplest realities which it exists to proclaim is the fact that God wills to reveal himself to men and that men are capable of receiving that revelation. Men can learn about God by reading the Bible, by studying the operation of natural law in the universe which he created, and in many other different ways. The Christian can do very much more than know about God; he can know him for himself. When Jesus died on the cross 'the veil of the temple was rent in twain from the top to the bottom.' [2] From earliest times Christians have regarded the rending of the temple veil as being symbolical of the fact that in the drama of man's redemption Jesus not only fulfilled but also abrogated the old covenant, and by his life-giving Death and Resurrection inaugurated the new covenant, whereby every man might come to God through Jesus Christ in a living and personal encounter. The spiritual life of the Christian may well be described as getting to know God, progress in the spiritual life as advancement in the knowledge of God, and the goal of the spiritual life, namely, the perfection which Jesus enjoined upon his followers, as the attainment of the knowledge of God in all the fullness of meaning which the term implies.

In the long history of Western Christendom it has frequently been the founders of Religious Orders who have contributed in a marked degree to the growth of the spiritual life in the midst of a pagan society or a hostile world. The richness and the variety

[1] Luke 2 : 15b.　　　　[2] Mark 15 : 38.

13

of spiritual gifts which the Benedictine, Jesuit, Franciscan, Carmelite and other Religious Orders have contributed to the spiritual heritage of the Christian Church are as inestimable as they are diverse. Yet it is important to remember that the words of St. Paul : 'There are diversities of gifts but the same Spirit' [3] have a particular application to the history of Christian spirituality. For, as Père Bouyer has observed, 'not a single holy founder or reformer of a religious order has ever had the intention of founding a particular spirituality, more or less departmentalized.' [4] It is equally invidious to infer, as some contemporary writings do, that there is one kind of spirituality for Religious, another for clergy, and another for the laity, for all are equally committed to live the Christian life with the context of their baptismal vows. To quote Père Bouyer again : 'It is not a question of denying that the different environments where one may be called to live, the different historical circumstances in which one may find oneself, the different vocations, each one bound up with what is irreducible in every one's personality, very legitimately and moreover, inevitably, cause the application of the Gospel to human life to vary. But the fact remains that there is, and there always will be, only one Gospel. On the other hand, in our epoch as in all epochs, there are people naïvely persuaded that humanity worthy of the name was born yesterday and that it no longer has anything in common (or not anything much that is worthy of attention) with the humanity of former times. But those who entertain such fancies soon appear, in fact, incapable of interest in what is the most fundamental in man, what is most permanent and what is most human as well. The champions of these "new men" who are not the human being of the Gospel are regularly revealed as tyrants and finally as murderers of the eternal man, the real man.' [5] It is to this man of all times, this real man, that the great

[3] I Cor. 12 : 4.
[4] L. Bouyer, *La Spiritualité du Nouveau Testament et des Pères*, 1960, p. 13.
[5] ibid. Translation mine.

masters of the spiritual life still speak despite the passing of centuries and the effects of social change; and no one with more lasting influence than Saint Benedict of Nursia.

Of the life of Saint Benedict, who has often been called 'the father of Western Monasticism,' but few details are known. He was born at Nursia in about A.D. 480, and was educated at Rome amid the licentiousness of contemporary society. About the turn of the century he withdrew to Subiaco, forty miles east of Rome, where he lived the hermit life, drawing much of his inspiration from Cassian, Basil the Great and Caesarius of Arles. Gradually a community grew up round him and within his lifetime some twelve monasteries were established in the vicinity with twelve monks in each, and with abbots appointed by himself. To this day the convent over the site of the cave which the saint inhabited is the principal house of the Cassinese Congregation of Primitive Observance, to which is attached the English province with abbeys at Ramsgate and Prinknash. Several years ago it was the present writer's privilege to go on pilgrimage to Subiaco and in the silence of the place where men have lived under Benedictine rule for nearly fifteen centuries it was not hard to realize how Saint Benedict came to view the life in community as that which is most suited to the majority of those whose vocation is to the monastic life, those whom he called in his Rule 'the strong race of the Cenobites.' [6] He continued to think of the hermit life as the harder and more exacting vocation and considered the Cenobitic life as a valuable part of the preparation of the hermit, as the rule explicitly states : 'The second [7] are the Anchorites or Hermits, that is those who not in the first fervour of their conversion,[8] but after long probation in a monastery, having learnt in association with many brethren how to fight against the devil, go out well-armed from the ranks of the community to the solitary combat of the

[6] Rule, Ch. 1.

[7] i.e., kind of monks.

[8] Latin. *conversatio*—evidently meaning someone who has just entered upon the monastic life.

desert. They are now able to live without the help of others, and by their own strength and God's assistance to fight against the temptations of the mind and body.' [9]

It was at Monte Cassino, where he moved in about 525, and not at Subiaco, that Saint Benedict finally evolved the pattern of community life lived under the three vows of stability, obedience and monastic virtue and with its regular rhythm of liturgical worship and private prayer, of study and manual labour. It was here, too, that he composed his famous Rule, whose influence was to be so great that the eighth to the eleventh centuries in Europe came to be known as 'the Benedictine centuries.' When he died in 550, he was buried in the same grave as his sister, Saint Scolastica, whom he used to meet once a year for the discussion of spiritual matters. His festival is observed on March 21st.

It is one of the curious paradoxes of history that, although the adoption of the Rule of Saint Benedict was so widespread and its influence so lasting, Saint Benedict himself 'legislated for a house, not an order, and there is, in fact, no evidence that any house explicitly adopted his Rule for its sole guide for a hundred years or more after his death.' [10] The monastery which the Rule envisages is a self-contained unit, kept economically self-sufficient through the manual labour of the monks and constitutionally autonomous under the rule of the abbot. The division of the monastic day as well as the organization of the monastery as a whole was developed to serve the Benedictine ideal, namely, the service of God in simplicity of life and in abstraction from the world. About four hours a day were to be spent in liturgical prayer, about four hours in meditative reading, the lectio divina, or prayer, and about six hours a day in manual work or domestic crafts. In an atmosphere of silence and within the context of absolute regularity, strict discipline and unvarying routine the Benedictine monk lives out his days in what the Prologue to the Rule terms 'a school of the Lord's service.' While drawing on the

[9] Rule, Ch. 1.
[10] M. Deanesly, *A History of the Medieval Church*, p. 18.

wisdom and experience of the past, the Founder turned away from the extreme physical austerity of the eremetical ideal of his day and prescribed for his monks such discipline as was consonant with a large measure of manual work, and suitably attuned to Western temperaments and needs. For example, the Night Office was to be said, but the Horarium was to be so arranged that the monks should have their sleep unbroken. It is noteworthy that the Benedictine monk is not required to take a vow of poverty as such, but it is impossible to fulfil the requirements of the Rule without living in the spirit of poverty. At the time the Rule was formulated, as far as material conditions were concerned, 'the life must have approximated, not to the rigours of the Egyptian hermits, but to the poverty of the Italian peasant of the day.' [11]

The penetrating influence of the Benedictine code of life can be explained in large measure by the fact that the comparative moderation and prudence of its requirements brought the fulfilment of them within reach of many. Dom David Knowles has observed that Saint Benedict evidently intended the 'preceptive portions of the Rule to be, as it were, the minimum standard of an evangelical life, which could be demanded of all, but which proficients could transcend while yet fulfilling, as a skilled musician transcends without transgressing, the laws of harmony.' [12]

During the 'Benedictine centuries' the Rule maintained a position of unique authority, for the pattern of monastic life based upon it was 'everywhere the norm and exercised from time to time a paramount influence on the spiritual, intellectual, liturgical and apostolical life of the Western Church.' [13] Although many other expressions of the Religious Life have since taken their place within the established traditions of Christian spirituality, and although social conditions have greatly changed since Saint Benedict's day, the Benedictine ideal has shown itself capable of

[11] op. cit., p. 39.
[12] D. Knowles, *The Monastic Order in England*, 1950, p. 10.
[13] ibid., p. 3.

B

being translated into the conditions of each passing century, within the Anglican as well as the Roman obedience. In a recent essay an Anglican Benedictine has observed that 'just as Saint Benedict followed the liturgical custom of the Church of his day, so have his successors. The Daily Conventual Mass, attended by all the community, as the centre of its life and self-offering, is now universal. The Divine Office, the "Work of God," has become part of the prayer of the whole Church. For many centuries now the Benedictine has known that he is called to pray both with the whole Church of God and in its name. He sees in this a major part of his calling to apostolic life. From this springs the leadership of Benedictines in the work of liturgical reform and the work for Christian unity.' [14]

It would appear that Saint Benedict himself remained a layman throughout his life, and his Rule originally assumed that its adherents would be laymen. Herein lies much of its present appeal, for the spirit of the Rule still has much to teach the Christian layman even if he is living out his vocation under the implications of his baptismal vows, without the additional obligations of Religious profession, for 'the spirit of the Rule . . . is above all a spirit of order and of the forming of nature to receive grace by way of gentle, steady growth. No reader can fail to remark how often the natural foundation, whether of the human family or of the purest inclinations of human nature, is taken as a basis for the higher order of things, and how often Saint Benedict uses, not the language of high spirituality, but that of everyday intercourse, describing the simplest, smallest actions; . . . the gentleness, the humanity, the equilibrium of his teaching, which passes so naturally from the discipline of manners to the discipline of soul. It is a spirit alien alike to an austerity which is merely material and to a barbarism which falls below the level of human dignity. . . . Imprecisions there are, and silences which later ages found it necessary to fill with words, but Saint Benedict

[14] Dom Robert Petitpierre, *Christian Spirituality To-day,* ed. Ramsey, 1961, p. 31.

never confuses charity with mere good nature, filial respect and obedience with human affection, peace and order with comfort and ease, measure and discretion with faint-heartedness and mediocrity, and through all vicissitudes the Rule has remained one of the great formative influences in the life of the Church. . . .' [15] The excerpts from the Rule which have been chosen for comment in the remainder of this chapter have been selected for their very wide, if not universal, application, in the hope that readers may be encouraged to turn to the Rule for themselves, as well as to some of the devout commentaries upon it, which have been written down the centuries by the spiritual sons of Saint Benedict.

That the Holy Rule makes no distinction between two kinds of Christian perfection, one for monks and nuns and one for Christian living in the world, is made clearly apparent by its essentially biblical character and outlook. The Prologue sounds the call to perfection in a sequence of biblical quotations and allusions which make it clear that the Benedictine understanding of the divine call to man and of man's response to it is grounded in the Scriptures : 'Up with us then at last, for the Scripture arouseth us, saying : "Now is the hour for us to rise from sleep." Let us open our eyes to the divine light, and let us hear with attentive ears the warning that the divine voice crieth daily to us : "To-day if ye will hear his voice, harden not your hearts." And again : "He that hath ears to hear, let him hear what the Spirit saith to the churches." And what doth he say? "Come, ye children, hearken unto me : I will teach you the fear of the Lord. Run while ye have the light of life, lest the darkness of death overtake you." ' [16] Not only are there frequent quotations from and allusions to Holy Scripture—Abbot Cuthbert Butler lists over 200 of them in the text of the Holy Rule—but the Benedictine life made the monk fully familiar with the Scriptures both through his daily Bible reading in his own study period and

[15] D. Knowles, op. cit., pp. 14–15.
[16] Prologue.

through the lections of the Monastic Breviary. The importance of the Bible as the foundation of the spiritual life is mentioned in the Rule itself : 'For what page or what utterance of the divinely-inspired books of the Old and the New Testament is not a most unerring rule of human life?' [17]

The Prologue to the Rule is itself a masterpiece of spiritual wisdom and insight. The opening sentences underline the essential importance of attentiveness, willingness and obedience on the part of him, 'whosoever thou mayest be that renouncing thine own will to fight for the true King, Christ, dost take up the strong and glorious weapons of obedience.' The next part of the Prologue, already quoted, is reminiscent of the eagerness, the excitement and the sense of urgency with which the first Christians entered upon the Christian warfare. That the Christian life is a warfare against evil is a metaphor beloved of spiritual writers from Saint Paul onwards, and it is a conception which pervades both the Prologue and the Rule. That ultimate victory is assured is the faith of the Christian who can rest confident in recollection of the fact that it is Christ himself who extends the invitation, who indicates the way of fruitfulness, and who brings the Christian at last to share in his sovereignty and to enter into the very presence of God himself : 'What can be sweeter to us, dearest brethren,' Saint Benedict enquires of his spiritual sons, 'than this voice of our Lord inviting us? Behold in his mercy the Lord showeth us the way of life. Let us, therefore, gird our loins with faith and the performance of good works, and following the guidance of the Gospel walk in his paths, so that we may merit to see him who has called us unto his kingdom.' [18] There is no suggestion in the Holy Rule that any amount of religious devotion could be thought of as a substitute for a blameless life. The Prologue explicitly states that 'the Lord daily expects our life to correspond with his holy admonitions. And the days of our life are lengthened and a respite allowed us for this very reason.'

[17] Ch. 73.
[18] Prologue.

Progress in the spiritual life can only be made after much patience and perseverance and the ultimate attainment of perfection will be the fruit of love and service, of discipline and suffering for Christ's sake. The whole purpose and goal of the spiritual life is expounded with incomparable beauty and simplicity in the concluding paragraph of the Prologue, and although it has special reference to those who are following the Benedictine vocation, it may be seen to apply in a very real sense to all who have taken upon themselves the yoke of Christ:

'Therefore must we establish a school of the Lord's service; in founding which we hope to establish nothing that is harsh or burdensome. But if, for good reason, for the amendment of evil habit or the preservation of charity, there be some strictness of discipline, do not be at once dismayed and run away from the way of salvation, of which the entrance must needs be narrow. But, as we progress in our monastic life and in faith, our hearts shall be enlarged, and we shall run with unspeakable sweetness of love in the way of God's commandments; so that, never abandoning his rule but persevering in his teaching in the monastery until death, we shall share by patience in the sufferings of Christ, that we may deserve to be partakers also of his kingdom. Amen.'

'As my Father hath sent me, even so send I you.' [19] The principle of authority is deeply rooted in the Gospel and in the organized life of the Church. Yet those who hold office and bear rule in the Church carry an authority which is meant to be expressed not in overlordship but in service, after the example and the precept of Jesus himself: 'And whosoever of you will be the chiefest, shall be servant of all. For even the Son of man came not to be ministered unto, but to minister, and to give his life a ransom for many.' [20] One of the longest and most outstanding chapters in the Rule is the second chapter, which describes 'What kind of man the abbot should be.' Whoever is called to bear authority in the Church of God as bishop, priest or Religious

[19] John 20: 21b.
[20] Mark 10: 44, 45.

superior, and whoever receives their ministrations and admonitions, will find much to ponder in the words of the Holy Rule:

'An abbot who is worthy to rule a monastery should always remember what he is called and realize in his actions the name of a superior. For he is believed to be the representative of Christ in the monastery, and for that reason is called by a name of his, according to the words of the Apostle: "Ye have received the spirit of the adoption of sons, whereby we cry, Abba, Father." Therefore the abbot ought not to teach, or ordain, or command anything which is against the law of the Lord; on the contrary, his commands and teaching should be infused into the minds of his disciples like the leaven of divine justice. Let the abbot remember always that at the dread Judgement of God there will be an examination of both these matters, of his teaching and of the obedience of his disciples. And let the abbot realize that the shepherd will have to answer for any lack of profit which the Father of the family may discover in his sheep. On the other hand, if the shepherd have spent all diligence on an unruly and disobedient flock and devoted his utmost care to the amending of its vicious ways, then he will be acquitted at the Judgement and may say to the Lord with the prophet: "I have not hid thy justice within my heart: I have declared thy truth and thy salvation; but they have despised and rejected me." And so at the last, for these sheep disobedient to his care, let death itself bring its penalty.'

Note has already been taken of the fact that the Benedictine pattern of life was that of a well-ordered and closely knit family. Parents and teachers and others who have to carry responsibility for others within the community, as well as clergy and Religious Superiors, will draw inspiration and encouragement from the Holy Father Benedict as he continues:

'For the abbot in his teaching ought always to observe the rule of the Apostle, wherein he says: "Reprove, persuade, rebuke." He must adapt himself to circumstances, now using severity and now persuasion, displaying the rigour of a master or the loving-kindness of a father. That is to say, that he must sternly rebuke the undisciplined and restless; but the obedient, meek, and patient, these he should exhort to advance in virtue. As for the negligent and rebellious, we warn him to reprimand and punish them. And let him not shut his eyes to the faults of offenders; but as soon as they begin to appear, let him, as he can, cut them out by the roots, mindful of the fate of Heli, the priest of Silo. Those of gentle disposition and good understanding should be punished, for the first and second time by verbal admonition; but bold, hard, proud and disobedient characters should be checked at the very beginning of their ill-doing by the rod and corporal punishment, according to the text: "The fool is not corrected with words"; and again: "Beat thy son with the rod and thou shalt deliver his soul from death." '

In the fourth chapter of the Rule entitled 'The Tools of Good Works,' the saint lists seventy-two short precepts and prohibitions, mostly quotations from the Old and New Testaments, which the seeker after perfection should strive to observe. The first nine, a recapitulation of the Ten Commandments, analyse the precept of charity which the ninth 'tool' defines as 'Not to do to another what one would not have done to oneself.' The next three deal with mortification, whose purpose is made plain in the tenth 'tool': 'To deny oneself, in order to follow Christ.' The next six 'tools' mention some of the most obvious active works of Christian mercy, such as visiting the sick and burying the dead. After counselling the disciple to 'avoid worldly conduct,' there follows that precept which may well be thought of as the very touchstone of Benedictine spirituality, namely: 'Nihil amori Christi praeponere.' (To prefer nothing to the love of Christ.) The next twelve 'tools' expound the Christian duty of charity towards one's neighbour, especially in difficult or exacting circumstances. The next group of 'tools' directs one's attention to the control of the senses and of the tongue, warns against pride, and reminds the disciple of the reality of the Four Last Things, death, judgment, heaven and hell. The forty-eighth 'tool' summarizes the whole ethos and context of the Benedictine way of life, without which no progress in the spiritual life can be made: 'In omni loco Deum se respicere pro certo scire.' (To know for certain that God sees one everywhere.) The remaining twenty-four 'tools' provide a variety of godly admonitions and prudent precepts. After a reminder 'never to despair of God's mercy,' the concluding paragraph of chapter four begins thus: 'Behold these are the tools of the spiritual craft. If we employ them unceasingly day and night, and on the Day of Judgement render account of them, then we shall receive from the Lord in return that reward which he himself has promised: "Eye hath not seen, nor ear heard, what God hath prepared for those that love him." '

The next three chapters, chapters five, six and seven, deal with three basic and cardinal essentials of the spiritual life, obedience, silence and humility. The chapter on obedience begins with the words: 'The first degree of humility is obedience without delay. This becometh those who hold nothing dearer than Christ.' For all Christians the first obedience is that given to God. For monks, the commands of the abbot are to be obeyed as Christ's. Outside monastic obligations the principle of obedience still persists for Christians living in the world, for God's will is constantly expressed to us both through our fellow-Christians and through those whom God would have us serve for Christ's sake. Of the significance of obedience and humility in the spiritual life of the ordinary Christian Dom Robert Petitpierre has recently written: 'Obedience is the attack on sin, because sin springs from self-will, which is the "laziness of disobedience." It follows then that every opportunity free from sin, and not contradicting the duties of our job in the world or the monastery, should be taken to do the will of someone else rather than our own will. In this we imitate our Lord. But above all we must put no thing and no one in the place of Christ, who says, "If ye love me, Keep *my* commandments." The habit of letting others choose the cinema, or the theatre, or the place on the bus, or the selection of food, can be very mortifying, and a very good thing too!

'Closely linked with this is the practice of humility. Humility is recognizing that we are worth nothing except what God has given us : and what God gives remains his property and we cannot claim it as our own. . . . But solid humility springs from the habit of looking at God.' [21]

No one can look at God unless he learns progressively to be silent in his own soul, and interior recollection is impossible, even for the most proficient, without some measure, and that usually a large one, of external silence. This point is emphasized by all spiritual writers in all ages and Saint Benedict is no exception, for the Rule speaks of 'the great value of silence,' and especially after Compline.

A very large part of the Rule, chapters 8–19, deals with matters affecting the Recitation of the Divine Office—the Opus Dei. This is indicative of the place that the liturgical prayer of the community occupies in the life of the Benedictine, or any other Religious Order. For nearly fifteen centuries the Benedictine Order has borne witness to that for which all Enclosed Communities stand, namely, that it is the vocation of some men and women, to devote their whole lives to the direct worship of God. Outside the Religious Life, the importance of joining in the Church's liturgical action and the observance of a Rule of life can hardly be overemphasized for those who would advance in the practice of the Presence of God. Private as well as corporate prayer is a basic essential of Christian spirituality. Although the Holy Rule says little explicitly about prayer, a great part of the monk's life was devoted to private, personal prayer. In chapter 20, however, the Rule recommends : 'If we wish to prefer a petition to men of high station, we do not presume to do it without humility and respect; how much more ought we to supplicate the Lord God of all things with humility and pure devotion. And let us be sure that we shall not be heard for our much speaking, but for purity of heart and tears of compunction. Our prayer, therefore, ought to be short and pure, unless it chance to

[21] Article in the *C.R. Quarterly Review,* Christmas 1961, p. 10.

be prolonged by the impulse and inspiration of divine grace.'

The twentieth century reader may have some difficulty in understanding what the Holy Father meant by 'pure prayer.' For guidance one may well turn again to Dom Petitpierre: ' "Pure" prayer is a technical term derived from the teaching of the Fathers of the Desert who use it to describe prayer which in our day we would call contemplation; i.e., having God and not self as its motive, and God himself and not any of his mysteries as its object. It is perhaps worth adding one further note on this. The life of contemplation is not divorced from hard work or from the regular recitation of the Church's liturgical prayer or from the various decisions dealing with the world around. It is a life which seeks God's will, and only God's will, in all these things. And contemplative prayer is not a series of wonderful lights and visions and understandings, but a dark and difficult piece of work, unless perhaps God's grace (for a very short time and on comparatively rare occasions) gives a flash of insight.' [22]

The spiritual life, whether monastic or otherwise, is a way of living which includes every aspect and activity of daily life. In the Benedictine monastery, where the monks are allowed a reasonable amount of food and drink, the cellarer has a very important responsibility to discharge on behalf of the whole community, and chapter 31 of the Rule is devoted to 'What kind of man the cellarer of the monastery should be.' Where the necessary substitutions of 'household' for 'monastery' etc. are made, the wise precepts of the Founder have a much wider application and much of his advice might be taken with great profit by the mother of a large family or any one in charge of an orphanage, school or any other Christian institution. For example:

'As cellarer of the monastery let there be chosen out of the community a man who is prudent, of mature character, temperate, not a great eater, not proud, not headstrong, not rough-spoken, not lazy, not wasteful, but a God-fearing man who may be like a father to the whole community. Let him have charge of

[22] op. cit., pp. 9–10.

everything; let him do nothing without the abbot's orders, but keep to his instructions. Let him not vex the brethren. If any brother happen to make an unreasonable demand, he should not vex him with a contemptuous denial, but reasonably and humbly refuse the improper request. Let him keep guard over his own soul, remembering always the saying of the apostle that "he that hath served well, secures for himself a good standing." Let him take the greatest care of the sick, of children, of guests, and of the poor, knowing without doubt that he will have to render an account for all these on the Day of Judgement. Let him look upon all the utensils of the monastery and its whole property as upon the sacred vessels of the altar. Let him not think that anything may be neglected. Let him neither practice avarice, nor be wasteful and a squanderer of the monastery's substance; but let him do all things with measure and in accordance with the instructions of the abbot.'

A high priority is given to the care of the sick in the Rule of Saint Benedict. The thirty-sixth chapter begins : 'Before all things and above all things care must be taken of the sick, so that they may be served in very deed as Christ himself; for he said : "I was sick and ye visited me"; and, "what ye did to one of these least ones, ye did unto me." ' With equal insistence the Rule continues : 'But let the sick on their part consider that they are being served for the honour of God, and not provoke their brethren who are serving them by their unreasonable demands.' Guests are to be treated in like manner. The fifty-third chapter of the Rule begins : 'Let all guests that come be received like Christ, for he will say : "I was a stranger and ye took me in." And let fitting honour be shown to all, but especially to churchmen and pilgrims.'

The last chapters of the Rule deal with the monks' relationships with each other, and the last but one chapter in particular, chapter 72, re-emphasizes how close is the monastic ideal of Saint Benedict to the New Testament ideal for all Christians :

' . . . There is a good zeal which separates from evil and leads to God and life everlasting. Let monks, therefore, exercise this zeal with the most fervent love. Let them, that is, "give one another precedence." Let them bear with the greatest patience one another's infirmities, whether of body or character. Let them vie in paying obedience one to another. Let none follow what seems good for himself, but rather what is good for another. Let them practise fraternal charity with a pure love. Let them fear God. Let them love their abbot with a sincere and humble affection. Let them prefer nothing whatever to Christ. And may he bring us all alike to life everlasting.'

In conclusion it is fitting to quote the judgment of Saint Gregory the Great, still as apt as when he wrote it fourteen centuries ago : 'The man of God, Benedict, among the many wonderful works that made him famous in this world, was also conspicuous for his teaching : for he wrote a Rule for monks, remarkable for discretion and rich in instruction. If any one desires to know more deeply the life and character of the man, he may find in the ordinances of that Rule the exact image of his whole government : for the holy man cannot possibly have taught otherwise than as he lived.' [23]

[23] *Dialogues,* Bk. II, ch. xxxvi, c. 593.

CHAPTER 2

SAINT BERNARD OF CLAIRVAUX
1090–1153

In these days when agnosticism, if not blatant disbelief, is both common and widespread, it is understandable, even though it may not be justifiable, for ardent Christian believers to look back with a certain wistfulness to the Middle Ages, which have often been called the 'ages of faith.' The Middle Ages were not, however, the idyllic Golden Age which they have sometimes been represented as being, for they were full of unrest, tension and exploitation. Yet they produced Saint Bernard of Clairvaux and other forceful masters of the spiritual life. The times in which Saint Bernard lived and laboured, agonized and wrote have been thus strikingly described by Daniel-Rops : 'Medieval humanity had great defects : violent, often cruel, often marked by debatable morals, it had, nevertheless, a great superiority over our humanity : it believed. It thought about God. Never for one moment did a man of the twelfth century envisage what has become the major heresy of our epoch, the diabolical rebellion of the creature who imagines he can do without the Creator. At that epoch, to use the blasphemous-sounding word of Nietzche, God was not "dead"; he was wonderfully alive.' [1] Therein lies undoubtedly much of the present appeal of Saint Bernard and much also of the explanation of the strength of the Cistercian way of life on both sides of the Atlantic to-day. The life and writings of Saint Bernard bear witness for our generation, as for his own, to the truth which the biblical writer had long ago proclaimed, 'God is not the God of the dead, but of the living.' [2]

Saint Bernard was born of noble and godly parents at Fon-

[1] H. Daniel-Rops: 'Quand un saint arbitrait l'Europe,' 1953, p. 113. Translation mine.

[2] Matthew 22 : 32b.

taines, near Dijon, in 1090. His father, Tescelin, was Lord of
Fontaines, and he ruled his estates and his family according to
lofty ideals, which he demonstrated by his own example. Bernard's
mother, Aleth, was a woman of great beauty and saintliness, and
she managed her household with great skill and efficiency. The
primary source of our knowledge of the life of Saint Bernard
comes from the *Vita Prima Bernardi,* recorded by his contemporaries, who were also his friends and admirers, William of
Saint Thierry, Arnold of Bonnevaux, and Geoffrey of Clairvaux.
William was abbot of Saint Thierry; Arnold was also a Benedictine abbot though he did not embrace the new reform, giving up
the black cowl for the white; and Geoffrey, who had once been
Bernard's secretary, eventually became fourth abbot in succession
to the founder. Their joint effort furnishes us not with a docu-
mented biography according to the standards of the modern his-
torian, but with a simple memoir of a man whom they loved well
and whose purpose of writing is made clear in the words of the
preface of William of Saint Thierry, which begins: 'If Thou
wilt grant me Thy favour and aid, O Lord, it is my aim to write
the life of Thy servant, and thereby to give honour and praise to
Thy Name. It was he whom Thou didst use to make the Church
of our day shine with grace and holiness, such as was common in
the days of the apostles but has seldom been seen since. I call
upon Thy love to help me in this work, for it is love of Thee
which inspires me to write it. It does not really matter how little
a man may feel the warmth of Thy love permeating his heart, for
when he sees such an outstanding witness to Thy honour and
glory casting its light upon the world, he must do all he can to
ensure that this light which Thou hast kindled is hidden from
none of Thy children.' [3]

Despite a devout childhood and an early awakening to the call
of God, Bernard did not embark upon the Religious Life without
opposition from his family and without those interior conflicts

[3] *St. Bernard of Clairvaux.* Translated by Geoffrey Webb and Adrian
Walker, 1960, p. 9.

and temptations which normally beset those who, in the full flower of their youth, make a whole renunciation of all that the world offers to receive the all that God gives in exchange. Having enlisted the help of his uncle Gaudry, who afterwards followed him to the cloister, Bernard eventually won over all his five brothers who also either accompanied him, or followed him, to Cîteaux. For it was to Cîteaux with its reputation for terrible austerity and extreme poverty, where, since 1098 under the leadership of Saint Robert, Saint Alberic and Saint Stephen Harding, a small group of men were attempting to reform the Benedictine Order and had established a house of new observance, that Saint Bernard betook himself in 1112 with thirty like-minded knights, his companions, to give themselves away to God. The Cistercian reform was 'nothing more or less than a return to the Rule of Saint Benedict, excluding those elements which had been added in the course of centuries. Everything was forbidden that was not explicitly authorized by the Holy Rule. Built by preference in marshy valleys, not on those towering heights favoured by the Cluniacs, the Cistercian abbeys were intended as homes of total renunciation. The habit of these monks consisted of a plain woollen tunic with scapular and cowl of the same material. Their diet admitted of no meat, fish, cooking fats, milk-products or eggs. They ate nothing except boiled vegetables; and from 14th September until Easter only one meal a day was allowed. They slept fully clothed on straw mattresses without covering. At midnight, roused by the monastery's one bell, the community rose for prayer and matins in a church that was of the utmost simplicity, without ornament of any kind. Above all, no monastery might accept gifts or tithes, and possessed no lands other than what was necessary to supply the monks with their food.' [4]

Until the arrival of Bernard and his companions, the young community had had a somewhat precarious existence, but, to quote the audacious phrase of M. Daniel-Rops, 'one might almost say

[4] H. Daniel-Rops, *Cathedral and Crusade,* Dent, 1957, pp. 128–9.

that Bernard's arrival had attracted God's attention to Clair-vaux.' [5] From now onwards the community began to increase. The appeal of such austerity and devotion was such that by the time Stephen Harding died in 1134, the Order possessed eighty-four houses, and by the time Saint Bernard himself died it possessed one hundred and fifty, and the number went on growing through the later Middle Ages. Even during his novitiate Bernard practised such severe mortification that it permanently under-mined his health and also stamped upon his life that pattern of sacrificial self-giving that was to characterize it till his death. Present-day Western society, which succeeds so largely in in-sulating itself against cold, privation and discomfort with the gadgets and appliances of a technological age, will often find Bernard's standards not only unrealizable of attainment, but in-comprehensible and marked by an excess of zeal. But true lovers are wont to be reckless in the expression of their devotion and the lovers of God are no exception.

In 1115, so soon after his entry into the Religious Life, Saint Bernard's sanctity and special gifts had already marked him out for leadership, and Stephen Harding sent him to establish a house of the Cistercian order, to which they gave the name of Clair-vaux, in the territory of the Count of Troyes. The secret and the appeal of Clairvaux in its 'golden age' was that it was inhabited by men who did not look upon the austerity and simplicity of their life as ends in themselves but as means whereby they were enabled to seek and to find that union with God which was the purpose of their lives and incidentally the theme of Saint Bernard's Sermons to them on the 'Song of Songs.' One can catch the spirit of Clairvaux from William of Saint Thierry's description of it: 'Men who come down from the hills around into the valley of Clairvaux for the first time, are struck by an awareness that God dwells there, for the simplicity and unpretentiousness of the buildings in the quiet valley betrays the lowly and simple life led by the monks for the sake of Christ. They find that the silence

5 op. cit., p. 82.

of the night reigns even in the middle of the day, although in this valley full of men there are no idle souls, and every one busies himself with the tasks entrusted to him. The only sound that can be heard is the sound of the brethren at work or singing their office in praise of God. Even usually worldly men are filled with much awe by this atmosphere of silence, with the result that not only are they slow to indulge in any idle or improper chatter, but keep their talking to a minimum.

'The loneliness of this place, hidden among the woods and closed in by the surrounding hills, was comparable to the cave where the shepherds found our holy father Saint Benedict, so closely did the monks of Clairvaux follow his form of life and style of dwelling. Although they all lived together, it may truthfully be said that they were all solitaries, for although the valley was full of men the harmony and charity that reigned there were such that each monk seemed to be there all by himself. We all know well that an unstable man is never alone even when he is by himself, and in the same way among men whose lives are under the stabilizing influence of the rule in silence and unit of purpose, the way of life itself helps to establish an inner solitude in the depths of the heart.' [6]

Yet by a strange paradox Bernard himself was destined to spend much of his time away from his monastery in the service of the Church at large, and was therefore forced to find his cloister in his own interior life. His willingness to give himself unsparingly to the needs and demands of nobles, kings, bishops and popes as well as to those of peasants and monks, women and travellers is explained by the fact that his life as a contemplative led him to seek not only the salvation of his own soul, but that of all mankind. To quote William of Saint Thierry again: 'His greatest desire was for the salvation of all mankind, and this has been the great passion of his heart from the first day of his life as a monk even to the day on which I am writing this, so that his longing to draw all men to God is like a mother's devoted care for her children.' [7]

[6] op. cit., pp. 59–60.   [7] op. cit., p. 45.

C

Only brief mention can here be made of the many missions in which he was engaged, so that it is impossible to give a complete picture of the variety of their range or the fullness of their extent. In 1128, for example, he was secretary to the Synod of Troyes, where he obtained recognition for the Rules of the new order of Knights Templar, Rules which he is said himself to have drawn up. In 1130 he sided with Innocent II against the claims of the rival pope, Anacletus, and for the next seven years he laboured unceasingly for the unity of the Church. By the force of his personality and the impact of his saintliness he was much in demand for the healing of schism, as for example at Aquitaine when that territory remained the only one on that side of the Alps to withhold its obedience to Innocent II. Bernard was not satisfied when Duke William finally said that he would give his obedience to Innocent but would not allow the bishops whom he had expelled to return to their sees, but he refused either to wrangle or to rely on the weight of intellectual arguments alone. Bernard's biographer, Arnold of Bonnevaux, tells us :

'And so the discussions went on, and Bernard left the contending parties to it, while he for his part, trusting in stronger weapons, went to say Mass. All those who were not under interdict went into the church, while the rest, with the Duke, stayed outside.

'After the consecration, and after the kiss of peace had been given, Bernard, acting no longer as a mere man, but as a priest who holds the Blessed Sacrament in his hands, took It outside to the Duke. With eyes no longer meek and persuasive, but blazing full of menace, he accosted the Duke with these words : "We came with humble requests, and you disdained them. All your people joined with us in beseeching you to let peace come back to your domains, but you despised them equally. Now see whom it really is that you persecute; it is the Lord, who is the Head of the Church, the Son of the Virgin. He is your judge. He is the one before whom every knee must bend, in heaven, earth and hell. Here is your judge, I say, and into his hands your soul must

34

one day come for judgement. Do you dare to despise him, as you have despised us and your people. Tell me, do you dare?"

'The people about him wept and prayed that God would enlighten the Duke to see his wrong, and how he should right it. Suspense held them all silent, waiting as if for some sign to come from heaven. Then the Duke, with trembling limbs, as if overawed by the majesty of Bernard's presence as he stood there holding the sacred Host, suddenly collapsed with fear. . . . Bernard then went up to him, and touching his feet told him to rise and listen to God's sentence.

' "The bishop of Poitou, whom you expelled from his church, is here," Bernard told him. "Go and be reconciled with him. Give him the kiss of peace and restore him to his rightful place. Likewise, bring all those others, among whom you have sown discord, once more into the unity of true brotherhood, and you will give glory to God and make satisfaction for the wrong you have done. Give your obedience to Pope Innocent, as all the rest of the Church does. Although you are chosen by God as a ruler over men, none the less you must obey his vicar upon earth."

'At this, the Duke could not utter a word, for he was wholly overcome by all that had passed that day. He went straight to the bishop of Poitou and gave him the kiss of peace. The hand that had thrown the prelate out, now restored him amid the exultations of the people. Meanwhile Bernard changed his tone and spoke familiarly and kindly as a father would, exhorting the Duke to keep his word and in no way violate the peace they had made that day, nor in any other way try God's patience by any bold and impious measure.' [8]

Although Saint Bernard believed that faith was more important than intellectual activity, that is not to say that he despised it. On the contrary, he is reputed to have remarked that 'It ill becomes a spouse of the Word to be stupid.' His literary output was enormous, and indeed astonishing, when it is remembered that he was following a contemplative vocation, travelling far and

[8] op. cit., pp. 92-3.

wide on enterprises of one sort and another, and was frequently severely ill and never well. More than three hundred sermons including the eighty-six which comprise his 'Commentary on the Song of Songs,' fourteen treatises including 'On the Love of God,' 'On the Knowledge of God,' 'On Grace and Free Will,' and his 'spiritual testament,' the 'De Consideratione,' as well as a huge and varied correspondence of which more than five hundred letters are still extant, reveal that Saint Bernard had a clear and penetrating grasp of theological problems, the ability to handle a polemical argument, an intimate knowledge of the Bible, and a fine eloquence which has seldom been surpassed.

Saint Bernard's passionate desire to defend the orthodox doctrines of the Western Church and the traditional methods of defining and expressing them has sometimes caused him to be represented by his detractors as an unbridled fanatic and even as a predecessor of the Inquisition. In this respect the most notable controversy in which he was engaged was with Peter Abelard, the brilliant dialectician whose teaching soon eclipsed that of his own teachers, and whose school of Saint Génevière at Paris, by the time he was forty, had five thousand pupils. Like his outstanding adversary, Bernard of Clairvaux, Abelard's literary activities were on a very large scale, but it was his *Christian Theology* which brought these two great minds of the twelfth century into head-on collision. In the light of history it can be seen that, apart from great differences of personality and outlook, the fundamental intellectual difference between them concerned the relation of faith to reason, and that their respective positions, which can now be seen to be complementary, were then thought of as violent alternatives. Saint Bernard saw Abelard's recourse to reason as a threat to dogma itself, and therefore felt bound to withstand him to his face at the Council of Sens in 1140. To every one's amazement Abelard refused to answer Bernard on that occasion, and appealed direct to Rome. This resulted, in the same year, in his condemnation and the public burning of his books.

Much can be learnt about Saint Bernard as well as about the

controversy in question from his numerous letters which survive. William of Saint Thierry had written to Saint Bernard, sending him a copy of *Christian Theology* and expressing his alarm concerning both Abelard's teaching and its wide dissemination, even to Rome itself. To which Saint Bernard had replied : 'In my opinion your misgivings are well called-for and reasonable. . . . As you well know, I am not in the habit of trusting much my judgement, especially in such grave matters as these, so I suggest that it would be worth our while to meet somewhere, as soon as we have an opportunity, and discuss the whole thing. But I do not think this can be arranged before Easter, lest we are distracted from that prayer that is proper to this season of Lent.' [9]

In due course Saint Bernard saw Abelard privately, and had hoped to have converted him, but in vain. Saint Bernard's continued reluctance to debate the matter in public, as well as the danger he believed the Church to be in through the propagation of Abelard's views, can be seen in his letter to the bishops of the Archdiocese of Sens.[10] After the Council of Sens, he wrote to Pope Innocent II a lengthy letter, describing what had taken place both then and previously describing the threat to the Church which he believed Abelard's teaching to be, and calling upon the Pope to suppress his heresies. 'His books have wings,' he wrote, 'and they who hate the light because their lives are evil, have dashed into the light thinking it was darkness. Darkness is being brought into towns and castles in the place of light; and for honey poison or, I should say, poison in honey is being offered on all sides to every one. His writings "have passed from country to country, and from one kingdom to another." A new gospel is being forged for peoples and for nations, a new faith is being propounded, and a new foundation is being laid besides that which has been laid. Virtues and vices are being discussed immorally, the sacraments of the church falsely, the mystery of the

[9] *Letters of St. Bernard of Clairvaux.* Translated and edited by Bruno Scott James, B.O.W., 1953, Letter no. 236, pp. 314–15.
[10] no. 237, p. 315.

Holy Trinity neither simply nor soberly. Everything is put perversely, everything quite differently, and beyond what we have been accustomed to hear. . . . But you, the successor of Saint Peter, will judge whether this man who has attacked the faith of Peter should find a refuge in the see of Peter. . . . God has raised up crazy heretics in your time that by your hand they may be crushed. . . . Catch for us, most loving father, the foxes that are destroying the vine of the Lord, while they are yet young; lest, if they should grow and multiply, what was not done for their extermination by yourself, may be the despair of those that come after you. Although now they are no longer so small or so few, but well grown and numerous, and only to be exterminated by your strong hand. . . . ' [11] After the condemnation of his writings Abelard came under the kindly protection of Peter the Venerable of Cluny until his pious death, after a long illness, in 1142. It is important to recognize that Saint Bernard's opposition to Abelard arose from his burning, conscientious desire to defend the Faith of the Church, and that, while he felt it necessary to demolish his adversary's opinions, he nevertheless remained in charity with him as a person. As soon as he heard of Abelard's mortal illness he hurried to his bedside, where Peter the Venerable watched the two men exchange the kiss of peace.

In so much as it was given to Saint Bernard to be, as it were, the conscience of the age in which he lived, it is not surprising to find him in 1145, the same year in which a Cistercian monk and former pupil of his became Pope Eugenius III, preaching the Second Crusade at Vézelay, with the full support of Louis VII, and with the same ardent zeal with which he undertook all his activities for the cause of God. Odo of Deuil records : 'In the end Bernard was tearing his own cowl into strips to make crosses for those clamouring about him. He spent the whole of his time preaching the crusade while he was in Vézelay. Despite the feebleness of his thin body, which was hardly sufficient to bear his strong soul about, he was everywhere, and the number of

[11] *Letters of St. Bernard of Clairvaux,* no. 239, pp. 317–20.

those bearing the cross was constantly increasing.' [12] His appeal was accompanied by many healing miracles which the saint was empowered to work, as on many other occasions, on the sick and crippled. Humanly speaking, it was a tremendous shock and disappointment to Saint Bernard when the news came that the Second Crusade had come to a disastrous end. He received the tidings, however, with his usual acceptance and trust: 'If it pleased God to save the souls of Western Christians from their sins, rather than save the bodies of Eastern Christians from the pagans, who are we to ask God, "Why hast thou done thus to us?" ' [13] When Saint Bernard was blamed for his own part in the Crusade he received it with meekness, after the example of the meekness of Christ, and in exemplification of his own words to Pope Eugenius III at the beginning of the treatise 'On Consideration': 'If we must choose between the lesser of two injustices, I had rather the calumny of men's tongues should fall upon us than be directed against God. I am happy enough if he wishes to use me as a shield, and I shall willingly let detraction and envenomed blasphemy come upon me, if I can avert it thus from God. I do not shrink from being humiliated, if I can prevent injury being done to his glory.' [14]

Saint Bernard was not only a monk but a man of affairs; not only a mystic but an administrator; not only a saint but a genius. The secret and the mainspring of his interior life and of his external works was his love for God, a love which embraced and absorbed all the powers of body, mind and soul. The essence of his teaching on the Love of God is distilled and preserved in the *De Diligendo Dei* ('On the Love of God'), which he wrote in answer to an enquiry from Haimeric, a Cardinal Deacon of the Roman Church, 'as to how God should be loved.' In the very beginning of the first chapter, Saint Bernard goes right to the heart of the matter when he states: 'The reason for our loving

[12] *vita prima.* op. cit., p. 110.
[13] ibid., p. 117.
[14] ibid., p. 117.

God IS God; and measure of that love there should be none.' [15] The rest of the treatise may be seen to be an exposition of this statement.

In the first five chapters, Saint Bernard dwells on themes which often resemble those of Saint Paul both in language and in thought. Speaking of God's claim upon our love he says: 'He surely merits much from us who gave himself to us, unworthy as we were: what better gift *could* he have given than himself? If, then, it is his claim we have in mind when asking, *Why should God be loved?* the first and foremost answer is, "Because he first loved us."' [16] After enumerating the good gifts that man receives from God as his Creator, he goes on to speak of God's love in redemption, and therefore to stress the motives that Christians have for loving God and which unbelievers lack: 'Believers, on the other hand, know well their utter need of Jesus and him crucified; and they, while they embrace and marvel at the love revealed in him, are overwhelmed with shame because they pay not back, in answer to such love and consolation, even the very little that they are.' [17] The believer cannot but ponder the greatness of such love, and pondering, must enquire: 'So great a love, shown by so great a Lord, how can one pay it back? Dust that we are, what recompense is it, even to give our whole poor selves to him? Was not that majesty the first to love? Do we not see him wholly bent on our salvation's work?' [18] The greatness of the debt the Christian owes to God is summed up in the words: 'By his first work he gave me to myself; and by the next he gave himself to me. And when he gave himself, he gave me back *my*self that I had lost. Myself for myself, given and restored, I doubly owe to him. What, though, shall I return him for *him*self? A thousand of myself would be as nothing in respect of him.' [19]

---

[15] *On the Love of God.* Tr. A Religious of C.S.M.V., Mowbray, 1950, p. 13.
[16] ibid., p. 14.
[17] ibid., p. 24.
[18] ibid., p. 36.
[19] ibid., pp. 41–2.

With Saint Bernard the question of merit and reward is no sterile theological debate, but the simple language of one whose theology as well as his language springs from a love whose ground is gratitude, and which seeks no other prize than love's fulfilment : 'God is not loved without reward, although he should be loved without reward in view. . . . Much more, the soul that loves God seeks for God, and wants no other prize.' [20] The action of God upon the soul is expressed, not in the academic terminology of the theology of grace, but simply thus : 'He kindles thy desire himself, who is himself its Goal.' [21]

One of the most striking features of the *De Diligendo Deo* is Saint Bernard's exposition of what he terms 'the four degrees of love' in chapters 8–11. He calls the first degree of love the love for self, and this includes the love of one's neighbour : 'A love both just and balanced will be yours, if you deny not to your brother's need what you refuse to your own base desires. The love of God extended thus becomes benevolence.' [22] But benevolence must be lifted on to the plane of supernatural charity : 'For our love of others to be wholly right, God must be at its root. No one can love his neighbour perfectly, unless it is *in God* he holds him dear.' [23] With his habitual frankness Saint Bernard declares that 'Man begins by loving, not for God's sake but for his own.' [24] Hence the second degree of love is described as 'the love of God for what he gives.' The third degree of love brings a man to the point where 'he loves purely and without self-interest' [25] and thus loves God for what he is : 'Love of the quality of God's own love is this, seeking no more its own but those things that are Christ's, even as he sought ours—or rather *us,* and never sought his own. . . . It is the love of God *for* God, not merely for oneself.' [26] Of the fourth degree of love the saint exclaims : 'Happy is he who can attain the fourth degree of

[20] *On the Love of God,* pp. 45 and 47.
[21] ibid., p. 53.
[22] ibid., p. 58.
[23] ibid., p. 59.
[24] ibid., p. 61.
[25] ibid., p. 62.
[26] ibid., p. 63.

love, and love *himself* only for God's sake.' [27] He admits, nevertheless, that this fourth degree of love is not normally attained in this life, but goes on to describe the final blessedness of those who eventually attain it: 'Now from henceforth do we possess for ever that fourth degree of love, when God is loved supremely and alone; for we no longer love ourselves save for his sake, and he himself becomes his lovers' Recompense, Reward eternal of eternal love.' [28]

One of the marked characteristics of Saint Bernard's devotion and one which influenced succeeding centuries in a variety of ways was his special devotion to the humanity of our Lord. Of this there is abundant evidence in his sermons on the 'Song of Songs.' For example, commenting on the text, 'A bundle of myrrh is my well-beloved unto me,' Saint Bernard includes the passage: 'As regards myself, I, brethren, from the beginning of my conversion, set myself . . . to tie up this bundle of myrrh for my individual needs, collected from all the cares and bitter experiences of my Lord, and to keep it always close upon my breast; in the first place of the privations of his infant years: then of the labours he underwent in preaching, his fatigues in journeying to and fro, his watchings in prayer, his fastings and temptations, his tears of compassion, the snares laid for him in discourse; and, lastly, of his perils among false brethren, of insults, spitting, blows, abuse, scorn, piercing by nails, and other such things, which he suffered for the salvation of our race, which in the gospel history, as in a wood, may abundantly be gathered. And, among so many branches of that fragrant myrrh, I think that cannot be passed over, of which he tasted when upon the Cross, nor that wherewith he was embalmed in the sepulchre. In the first of these he applied himself to the bitterness of my sins, in the second he pronounced the future incorruption of my body. As long as I live I will proclaim loudly the abundance of the graces which come from these; I will never forget those mercies,

[27] *On the Love of God,* p. 64.
[28] ibid., p. 76.

since it is by them I have been restored to life.' [29] From this passage too, it is apparent that Saint Bernard stood at the junction of the centuries, for he used much the allegorical method of interpreting the Scriptures beloved of the Early Fathers of the Church, and his writings are also studded with personal and autobiographical references which anticipate so much of the self-revelation of later centuries, of Richard Rolle and of the Lady Julian, to take but two examples.

Associated with his devotion to the Humanity of Jesus was his devotion to the Holy Name, a devotion which acquired great popularity at this period. Works of art often demonstrate how far a particular devotion is typical of the age, and the medieval period is rich in examples. To take but one example : M. Daniel-Rops draws attention to a window in the basilica of Notre-Dame du Sacré Coeur at Issoudun, which shows 'our Lord and Saint Bernard standing face to face; and in order to express their mutual love, the artist has written above the Heart of Christ the one word "Bernard," and on the White Monk's breast the Holy Name.' [30] In St. Bernard's *Commentary on the Song of Songs* Sermon 15 is devoted to expounding 'In what manner the Name of Jesus is a salutary medicine to faithful Christians in all adversities.' Saint Bernard demonstrates how the Name of Jesus both expresses his power and goodness and becomes the means of salvation. The greater part of his exposition unfolds the text of the psalmist : 'Thy name is as oil poured forth.' He says that the Holy Name is compared to oil because both give light, food and medicine. He then goes on to examine each of these qualities separately, in a famous passage which indicates why the well-known hymn, 'Jesu dulcis memoria' (Jesu, the very thought is sweet) has been traditionally ascribed to him, though most modern commentators now repudiate that tradition. 'Whence,' enquires Saint Bernard, 'do you suppose so bright and so sudden a light

[29] *Cantica Canticorum.* Tr. and ed. Samuel J. Eales, Sermon XLIII, p. 268.
[30] op. cit., p. 90.

43

of faith has been kindled in the whole world, except by the preaching of the Name of Jesus? Is it not by the light of this sacred Name that God has called us into his marvellous light. . . . But the Name of Jesus is not only light; it is also nourishment. Do you not feel spiritually strengthened as often as you meditate upon it? What enriches the mind of the thinker as does the Name of Jesus? What so restores exhausted powers, strengthens the soul in all virtues, animates it to good and honourable conduct, fosters in it pure and pious dispositions? Dry and tasteless is every kind of spiritual food, if this sweet oil be not poured into it; and insipid, if it be not seasoned with this salt. . . . As honey to the mouth, as melody in the ear, as a song of gladness to the heart, is the name of Jesus. But it is also a medicine. Is any of you sad? Let Jesus come into your heart; let his Name leap thence to your lips, and behold, when that blessed Name arises, its light disperses the clouds of sadness, and brings back serenity and peace. Is any falling into crime? or even, in his despair, rushing upon death? Let him call upon that life-giving Name; does he not speedily begin to breathe again and revive? . . . Who, when in fear and trembling in the midst of dangers, has called upon that Name of power, and has not found a calm assurance of safety, and his apprehensions at once driven away? Where is the man who, when labouring under doubt and uncertainty, has not had the clear shining of faith restored to him by the influence of the Name of Jesus? Or who has not found new vigour and resolution given to him at the sound of that Name full of help, when he was discouraged by adversities, and almost ready to give way to them? Those are the diseases and ailments of the soul, and for them this is the remedy. . . . Nothing is so powerful as the Name of Jesus to restrain the impulse of anger, to repress the swelling of pride, to cure the wound of envy, to bridle the impulse of luxury, and extinguish the flame of fleshly desire; to temper avarice, and to put to flight ignoble and impure thoughts. For, when I utter the Name of Jesus, I set before my mind, not only a Man meek and humble in heart, moderate, pure,

44

benign, merciful, and, in short, conspicuous for every honourable and saintly quality, but also in the same individual the Almighty God, who both restores me to spiritual health by his example, and renders me strong by his assistance. All these things are said to me when the Name of Jesus is pronounced.' [31]

Closely connected with medieval devotion to the humanity of Christ is the same epoch's devotion to his blessed Mother, and both are inseparable from Saint Bernard. The Mother of his Lord was never far from his thoughts, and it has been suggested that he was the first to call her 'our Lady,' a title borrowed from the language of chivalry. The saint's veneration for the Virgin Mother sprang from the fact that in God's dealings with her and in her response, he saw the workings of divine love. In Sermon 29 on the 'Song of Songs' Saint Bernard says : 'There is still another, a chosen arrow; it is the love of Christ, which not only pierced the soul of Mary, but transfixed it from side to side, so that it left no part of that virgin heart empty of that love, but she loved with all her heart, all her soul, and all her strength, and was full of grace. Or perhaps it may be thus, that it transpierced her, in order to penetrate even to us, and that we might all receive of that fullness; that she might be the mother of charity, of which God, who is Love, is the Father; that she might bring forth and set her tabernacle in the sun, that the Scripture might be fulfilled, which says : "I will give thee for a light to the Gentiles, that thou mayest be my salvation to the ends of the earth" (Isa. 49 : 6).' [32] There are two other points concerning the saint's devotion to Mary which are worthy of mention. In keeping with the usage of patristic tradition we find the term 'Mother' used for the Church or for sanctifying grace, and not for Mary when she is addressed directly. Secondly, Saint Bernard's devotion to her did not extend beyond what Holy Scripture might warrant. When, for example, the Canons of Lyons had instituted a feast in honour of the Conception of the Blessed Virgin Mary, Saint

[31] *Cantica Canticorum,* Sermon 15, pp. 83–4.
[32] ibid., p. 191.

Bernard wrote to them, remonstrating with them on the grounds that there was no evidence for it in Scripture, the Fathers, or the tradition of the Church, and saying that, in any case, they should first have consulted the Holy See.[33]

One of the most important considerations in the history of Christian spirituality is the fact that Saint Bernard introduced into the thought and language of Christian devotion the theme of the soul espoused to Christ, a theme which was to become an integral part of Christian mysticism, and which was to inspire much lyrical poetry throughout the centuries. Saint Bernard's *Commentary on the Song of Songs* derives from a wholly allegorical interpretation of the Old Testament book. The imagery of the Canticle is so employed that Saint Bernard's use of the Bridegroom metaphor sometimes envisages Christ as the Bridegroom of the Church, a thoroughly biblical and patristic conception, and at other times as the Bridegroom of the soul. Commenting on the text, 'Arise, my love, my fair one, and come away' (Cant. 2 : 13), Saint Bernard begins Sermon 61 with these words : 'The Bridegroom manifests his great affection by repeating the words of affection. For repetition is a sign expressive of affection.' [34] Commenting on the words which follow he continues : 'Take heed that you bring chaste ears to this discourse of love; and when you think of these two who are its subject, remember always that not a man and a woman are to be thought of, but the Word of God and the devout soul. And if I shall speak of Christ and the Church, the sense is the same, except that under the name of the Church is specified not one soul only, but the unity, or rather the unanimity, of many souls.' [35] The imagery of the spiritual marriage depicts the blessedness of the final union of the soul with God, which all writers of the spiritual life understand to be its final goal. In the words of Saint Bernard : 'A great Bridegroom, then, will present himself thus to great souls; and he will treat them

[33] op. cit. Letter no. 215, pp. 289–93.
[34] ibid., p. 366.
[35] ibid., p. 367.

magnificently, sending them his light and his truth; leading them on and conducting them at length to his holy mountain and into its tabernacles, so that one thus blessed may say : "He that is Mighty hath done to me great things" (Luke 1 : 49); his "eyes shall see the King in his beauty" (Isa. 33 : 17); going before him towards oases in the desert, in which bloom the fragrant roses, and the lilies of the valleys, where are the pleasant shades of gardens, the gushing of silver fountains, the storehouses filled with all good things, the odour of perfumes, and lastly, the hidden precincts of the chamber of the King.' [36]

So assuredly did the contemporary Church recognize the sanctity of one of the greatest of her sons that Bernard of Clairvaux was canonized in 1174, only twenty-one years after his death. Nearly eight hundred years later, it is still the judgment of posterity that it is 'difficult to name any other saint in the history of the Church whose influence, both on the public life of an epoch and on the consciences of a multitude of individuals, was during his lifetime so profound and so pervasive.' [37]

[36] Letter no. 215, p. 213.
[37] D. Knowles, op. cit., p. 217.

CHAPTER 3

SAINT FRANCIS OF ASSISI
1181–1226

AMID the galaxy of saints who have mirrored Christ in the world
by the purity and holiness of their lives, none makes a greater
appeal than the Poverello, the Little Poor Man of Assisi. Yet the
nature of his appeal is frequently misunderstood and he is ad-
mired and extolled not only by Christians of all traditions but
also by many who revere him as a humanist, a pantheist or as a
rebel against authority within the Church, three roles which he
would certainly have repudiated with horror. To appreciate those
qualities in Saint Francis of Assisi which cause him to stand out
as one of the greatest masters of the spiritual life one cannot do
better than listen to the warning note uttered by one of his
spiritual sons in the introduction to the current pilgrimage book-
let offered to the present-day visitor to Assisi, for what he says
about Assisi is equally true of the appeal and charm of the saint
himself :

'. . . May I offer a word of warning, for there is a danger
lurking in the very beauty of this place.

'The art and natural beauty of Assisi are indeed fascinating to
the visitor, but if we stop short at them, we miss the mysterious
secret which lies hidden behind the exterior loveliness. To stand
lost in admiration of the splendour of the sunset over the valley
of Spoleto is not sufficient for the understanding of Assisi; neither
is it sufficient to come here to study the works of great artists and
different styles as we may do in any picture gallery. Those who
only do this, miss the soul of Assisi.

'Seven hundred years ago Assisi was the scene of one of the
most wonderful of human adventures. A man who had spent his
youth singing the praises of what seemed to him high ideals,

suddenly saw these dashed to the ground, and his steps were turned in an opposite direction.

'But the song never died on his lips, nor did joy die in his heart. He showed his fellow men that he had found the secret of happiness. Not only the memory, but a living sense of this adventure has been preserved in this unique city.

'Assisi guards the secret of Saint Francis; here his spirit lives, and to find and possess this spirit is the highest privilege offered to those who come here. In order to capture it we must get away from superficial curiosity; we must not even be held by the beauty which surrounds Assisi, nor by the art of Cimabue, Giotto and Simone Martini, for all these are only means by which we may penetrate into the sublime soul of Francis, steps by which we may reach him. Some people may draw near to him simply by looking at the stones which were the witnesses of his life.'

If one cannot, as the present writer was privileged to do, look at 'the stones which were the witnesses of his life,' one can enter into the spirit of that life by meditating on a well-known passage of the fifteenth century work, *The Imitation of Christ*, attributed to Thomas à Kempis, a passage which might well have been written with Saint Francis in mind :

'Jesus has many who love his Kingdom in Heaven, but few who bear his Cross. He has many who desire comfort, but few who desire suffering. He finds many to share his feast, but few his fasting. All desire to rejoice with him, but few are willing to suffer for his sake. Many follow Jesus to the Breaking of Bread, but few to the drinking of the Cup of his Passion. Many admire his miracles, but few follow him in the humiliation of his Cross. Many love Jesus as long as no hardship touches them. . . .

'Oh, how powerful is the pure love of Jesus, free from all interest and self-love! Are they not all mercenary, who are always seeking comfort? . . . Where will you find any one who is willing to serve God without reward?

'Seldom is any one so spiritual as to strip himself entirely of self-love. Who can point out any one who is truly poor in spirit

49

D

and entirely detached from creatures? His rare worth exceeds all on earth. If a man gave away all that he possessed, yet it is nothing. And if he did hard penance, still it is little. And if he attained all knowledge, he is still far from his goal. And if he had great virtue and most ardent devotion, he still lacks much, and especially the "one thing needful to him." And what is this? That he forsake himself and all else, and completely deny himself, retaining no trace of self-love. And when he has done all that he ought to do, let him feel that he has done nothing.

'Let him not regard as great what others might esteem great, but let him truthfully confess himself an unprofitable servant. For these are the words of the Truth himself : "When you shall have done all those things that were commanded you, say, We are unprofitable servants." Then he may indeed be called poor and naked in spirit, and say with the Prophet, "I am alone and poor." Yet there is no man richer, more powerful or more free than he who can forsake himself and all else, and set himself in the lowest place.' [1]

The remainder of this chapter will hope to show how apt a commentary this passage provides upon the life and devotion of the saint. The literature about Saint Francis is vast. Among the early sources the most important are the collection of the saint's own few writings, consisting mainly of two Rules, his Testament, some letters, exhortations and prayers; many early legends including the *Legend of the Three Companions,* the *Mirror of Perfection,* and the *Little Flowers of Saint Francis;* the two 'Lives' of Celano and that of Saint Bonaventura. The problem of the relations between the various sources and that of their historicity in the modern sense of the word need not detain us here. There is a large body of literature in all languages, dealing with such problems and especially of 'Lives' of the saint written in compliance with modern standards of biographical writing, though some of them, admittedly, have some affinity with the

[1] Thomas à Kempis, *The Imitation of Christ,* ed. Leo Sherley Price, Penguin Books, 1952, p. 82.

historical novel. Some of the important works in English are listed in the bibliography.

The main details of the life of Saint Francis are well known. To an amazing extent the places associated with his life, after seven centuries, not only cherish his memory, but enshrine his spirit. Not only at Assisi but at Saint Damian's and at the Carceri, at Fonte Colombo, Grecchio and Poggio Bustone, at Gubbio and La Verna, one can still catch the spirit of his familiar and well-remembered greeting: 'Pax et bonum,' 'Peace and well-being,' or else, 'The Lord give you peace.'

As the son of one of Assisi's richest and most influential citizens, the cloth-merchant Pietro Bernardone, Francis enjoyed a youth that was marked by gaiety, impulsiveness and a sense of adventure. Perhaps the first shadow to fall across this care-free existence was when Francis, fighting with the men of Assisi against the men of the neighbouring city of Perugia, was taken prisoner at Ponte San Giovanni and spent a year, 1202–3, in prison at Perugia, where his eager spirit chafed under the restrictions of confinement and his physical health was severely undermined. The *Legend of the Three Companions* tells how Francis did not rest until he had restored harmony between his fellow prisoners and another prisoner who had made himself so unpopular as to have been ostracized by them. Many times during his life he was to play the part of reconciler, sometimes between the members of his own beloved Order, sometimes between querulous citizens, as well as in his efforts to pacify the Sultan, or to end a violent dispute between the Bishop and the Governor of Assisi. The following prayer, beloved of many Christians amid the tensions of life in the world, well expresses the self-effacing, reconciling spirit of Saint Francis, which is the spirit of divine charity itself :

> *Lord, make me an instrument of your peace;*
> *Where there is hatred, let me sow love,*
> *Where there is injury, pardon,*

Where there is doubt, faith,
Where there is despair, hope,
Where there is darkness, light,
Where is sadness, joy.
O Divine Master, grant that I may not so much seek
To be consoled, as to console,
To be understood, as to understand,
To be loved as to love,
                    for
It is in giving, that we receive,
It is in pardoning, that we are pardoned,
It is in dying, that we are born to eternal life.

The *Legend of the Three Companions* makes it clear that from the time when he set out from Assisi in 1205 to join the army of Walter de Brienne, who was fighting on the Pope's behalf in southern Italy and whereby Francis hoped to fulfil his great ambition of becoming a knight, until the morning of St. Matthias' Day, February 24th, 1206, he passed through a time of striving and questioning, which was marked by dramatic events and vivid spiritual experiences on the one hand, and by hardness, loneliness and uncertainty on the other. The first crisis came immediately. Hardly had he set out, the party having got no farther than Spoleto, than Francis became aware of a voice asking him during the night : 'Which is it better to serve, the master or the servant?' To which he replied, 'the master, of course.' 'Then why do you serve the servant instead of the master, the poor instead of the rich?' Realizing from whence came the voice, Francis replied, 'Lord, what do you want me to do?' 'Go home,' came the answer, 'there you will be told what to do.'

It must have taken great courage for Francis Bernardone to turn his back on the life of adventure and romance that the Apulian expedition offered, and to return so soon to his home town, where he must have expected to be treated with mockery and derision. For a time, however, he appears to have been as popular as ever with the youth of Assisi, resuming his old life of gay extravagance and irresponsible escapades. It was while he was taking a leading part in one of such revels that his companions suddenly found him missing from their company, and, on returning to look for him, they found him sitting in a trance-like state. Whereupon they asked him : 'What's wrong with you? Have you fallen in love?' 'Yes,' he said, 'I have; and she is nobler, richer and lovelier than any other.' His friends could hardly have been expected to do anything but laugh at him, and to treat the incident lightly. For Francis, however, it was no laughing matter. The hound of heaven was in pursuit, and the nature of his vocation, to take, as he afterwards liked to say, Lady Poverty as his bride, was becoming increasingly clear.

The realization of what God wanted him to do was impressed upon the sensitive soul of Francis by a number of other episodes. Not only did he begin to withdraw from the noisy, pleasure-seeking life of his friends, to spend more time in solitude and prayer, and to distribute much wealth to the church and the poor, but he went on a pilgrimage to Rome. Acting with the impulsiveness that was always one of his most marked characteristics, Francis exchanged clothes with a beggar on the steps of Saint Peter's and sat there for a whole day, experiencing for himself the hunger and the humiliations of the destitute. On his return to Assisi his love for the poor and his desire to identify himself with them continued to grow, and were put to the test most severely on the day when, meeting a leper on the road to Assisi, he overcame his fear and disgust, dismounted from his horse, gave the leper an alms, and kissed him. From then on, he spent his time increasingly with the lepers, finding joy in serving them as he grew to recognize our Lord in the sick and the poor.

The next step towards his entire submission to the Will of God and his total acceptance of his new-found vocation was taken when he was kneeling before the Byzantine-style crucifix in the crumbling church of Saint Damian's. 'Francis, don't you see that my house is falling down?' came the gentle voice from the

Cross. 'Go and build it up again.' 'Yes, Lord,' he replied, 'I will.' It is well-known how Francis incited his father's anger by selling a bolt of his cloth in his usual impulsive way to procure the money he wanted to restore the church, and how he soon realized that he was meant to restore the church with his own hands. Pietro Bernardone's growing incomprehension, bewilderment and anger at his son's changed and astonishing behaviour not only caused Francis to go and take refuge with the old priest at Saint Damian's, whence he went out with his begging bowl and forced himself to eat the scraps which people gave him, but led to the dramatic public scene in the bishop's palace, when the bishop was called upon to arbitrate between the enraged Pietro Bernardone and his son. In sorrow and anger the old man disinherited the son who had been his pride and joy and demanded back the money. 'Not only the cash,' cried Francis, 'you might as well take my clothes too! I will now no longer say, "My father Pietro Bernardone, but our Father who art in heaven." ' As the father gathered up the money and the clothes and walked out, the bishop, with a kindly gesture, wrapped his cloak around the all but naked youth. Perhaps he was already beginning to realize what Francis was still to find out, that Francis was destined to restore the church with more than stone and mortar.

Having from this hour taken Holy Poverty as his bride, Saint Francis spent the next few months begging for stones with which to finish restoring Saint Damian's, then Saint Peter's in the town of Assisi, and finally the little chapel of Saint Mary of the Angels, or the Portiuncola, which he was to love most of all and which, despite its present splendour, is one of the holiest places in the world. Saint Francis, even now, was not yet finally aware of the direction that the rest of his life should take, in obedience to the call of God and affianced to Lady Poverty. Surely it was to be something more significant than rebuilding small, forgotten churches. St. Francis found the answer to the spiritual struggles of the past year or so in the words of the Gospel as he heard Mass in the Portiuncola on the Feast of Saint Matthias, 1206.

'As ye go, preach, saying, The kingdom of heaven is at hand. Heal the sick, cleanse the lepers, raise the dead, cast out devils; freely ye have received, freely give. Provide neither gold, nor silver, nor brass in your purses, nor scrip for your journey, neither two coats, neither shoes, nor yet staves; for the workman is worthy of his meat.' Saint Francis heard these words as if they had been written for him alone. As soon as the Mass was over he called out in exultation: 'This is what I have been wanting, this is what I have been seeking; this is what I long with all my heart to do.'

From this day forward the imitation of Christ meant for Saint Francis an unswerving and an unbroken obedience to the literal precepts of the Gospel. The rest of his life becomes a unity. Having overcome by faith all fear of the consequences, there is no limit to the power of love, Love given and Love received. The manner in which he lived for the rest of his life in utter poverty and simplicity; the alternating periods of prayer and penance, of preaching and evangelism, of external works and of interior contemplation; the establishment and life of the Order of Friars Minor as well as the troubles within it; the extremes of adulation and misunderstanding which he received from his own brethren, from high ecclesiastics and from ordinary folk; the appeal of the life of poverty which attracted Saint Clare and so many others to devote themselves to one or other of the three Franciscan Orders; his sense of kinship with all creatures; his devotion to the Passion of Christ and his receiving of the Stigmata; the alternating sadness and joy of the last years of his life, his last illness and his holy death; the enormous growth and influence of the Franciscan ideal down the centuries; and the lasting appeal of his personality and of his sanctity—all these things sprang from and can be explained by the saint's utter fidelity to the Gospel. As he and his first companions, Bernard of Quintavalle, Peter of Cattaneo and the others began to fashion their lives together, everything was modelled upon the literal words of the Gospels. Wishing to be no richer than their Lord in his poverty, they, who had been rich and influential, not only gave away all their possessions to the poor, but chose to be homeless in honour of him who said, 'The foxes have holes, and the birds of the air have nests; but the Son of man hath not where to lay his head' (Matt. 8: 20). When his companions and followers became so numerous that it became necessary to formulate a Rule, Saint Francis composed it with the words of the Gospel as its basis. It was this simple Rule, the original format of which has unfortunately been lost, which Saint Francis composed at Rivotorto and on which Pope Innocent III finally set the seal of his oral approval, after he had a dream in which he had seen the Lateran Basilica falling down and Francis with his own strength holding it up.

As has already been emphasized, the corner-stone of the Franciscan ideal was the life of poverty, not merely the spirit of poverty, but actual poverty, sometimes even to the point of destitution. What poverty meant to Saint Francis is expressed in many of the early legends and in the saint's own writings. The Fioretti describes one occasion when, on one of their preaching tours, Saint Francis and Brother Masseo placed some bread which they had begged on a stone beside a fountain and the following dialogue ensued:

'And Saint Francis, seeing that the pieces of bread which Brother Masseo had were larger and better than his own, had great joy, and spoke thus: "O Brother Masseo, we are not worthy of so great a treasure." And as he repeated these words several times, Brother Masseo answered him, "Father, how can this be called treasure, when we are in such great poverty, and lack the things of which we have need; we, who have neither cloth, nor knives, nor plates, nor porringer, nor house, nor table, nor manservant, nor maidservant?" Then said Saint Francis: "And this is what I call a great treasure, that there is nothing here provided by human industry, but everything is provided by Divine Providence, as we may see manifestly in this bread which we have begged, in this stone which serves so beautifully for our table, and in this so clear fountain : and therefore I desire that we should pray to God, that he would cause holy poverty, which is a thing so noble that God himself was made subject to it, to be loved by us with our whole heart." And when they had said these words, and they had made their prayer, and partaken for bodily refreshment of the pieces of bread, and drunk of the water, they arose, and went on their way to France.'

It was the custom of Saint Francis to summon the brethren twice a year for a general chapter meeting. At one of these gatherings at the Portiuncola in 1219 little huts of matted straw had been put up to accommodate the brethren, from which it became known as the 'Chapter of the Mats.' At that meeting Cardinal Ugolino, who was at the papal court at Perugia, was present, and it is believed that Saint Dominic and seven of his own Order were there too. There were about five thousand Friars Minor present from many European countries, all committed to the same strictness of life under the vows of poverty, chastity and obedience. In view of the tremendous growth of the Order within the space of a few years, it is pertinent to enquire whether the particular conditions of thirteenth century Europe were peculiarly propitious to its growth. At the beginning of the century the entrenched position of monasticism was being questioned. Men were wondering whether the monastic rules were really necessary, whether the gospel applied to life were not sufficient, whether other people besides monks were able to aspire to a high degree of spirituality. In such conditions, says Dom Vandenbroucke, 'the old monastic life no longer satisfied a certain number of people, those who were looking for a spiritual support adapted to their circumstances and to their conception of the perfect life, or those who were craving for a purer evangelism and for a more energetic reaction against abuses, especially against the wealth of the monasteries and the higher clergy, and again those who wished to get to grips with the new scientific tasks.

'The Franciscan springtime came into being in this context, as the providential response to these aspirations rising from the depths of the Christian soul. Poverty appeared as a remedy, if not *the* remedy. Poverty was for all, poor and rich, clergy and laity, the living reminder of what Christ expected of them.' [2]

Nevertheless it was the interpretation of the meaning of poverty which brought dissension into the Order during the lifetime of Saint Francis, which caused him to rewrite the Rule albeit with a sense of great disappointment and misgiving, and which brought about tensions and divisions within the Order after his death, resulting finally in the establishment of three independent Franciscan families, the Friars Minor, numbering 25,848, the Friars Minor Conventual, numbering 3,600, and the Friars Minor Capuchin, numbering 14,225 in 1955.[3] It is no part of our present purpose to follow what the Bishop of Ripon calls 'the well-worn track of Franciscan history during the first century of its existence,' but a comment from this contemporary authority on Franciscan studies may help us to see the Franciscan ideal of poverty in perspective. 'The characteristic feature of the way of life associated with Saint Francis of Assisi is poverty. Absolute poverty, both individual and corporate, was what was demanded of all who followed him. He thus went much further than the traditional monastic vow of poverty, which, while it denied to the monk any personal property, allowed the community to be comparatively wealthy. The Franciscan was allowed nothing. He was to earn his keep by manual work, and if that failed he was to resort to "the table of the Lord" and beg his food from door to door.

'This ideal was all right so long as those who tried to live by it were a small band of zealots under the personal and powerful influence of Saint Francis himself. It became impracticable when the little brotherhood had grown into a great religious order in all parts of the world. The story of the Franciscan Order is the story of an attempt to be loyal to an ideal which became more and more impossible.' [4]

[2] *La Spiritualité du Moyen Age*, Pt. 2, 1961, pp. 345–6. Translation mine.
[3] Pontifical Year Book, 1955.
[4] S.P.C.K., *View Review*, vol. 12, no. 4, p. 20.

Mention has already been made of the chapel of St. Mary of the Angels or the Portiuncola, which Saint Francis restored with his own hands. It had belonged originally to the Benedictine monks of Mount Subasio, who gave it to Saint Francis to make it the centre of his new foundation, tiny and isolated as it was. Here he came to live and here he requested to be brought when he was dying. The great basilica which now encloses the Porti-uncola is connected by a cloister with various spots hallowed by memories of the saint. The statue of Saint Francis with the doves recalls the occasion when he met a youth who was taking some turtle doves to be sold. The youth responded to the saint's appeal not to let them go into the hands of those who might be cruel to them and gave them to Saint Francis. Whereupon the saint remonstrated with the turtle doves for allowing themselves to be caught and then proceeded to make nests for them, whom he loved on account of their gentleness and innocence. In the rose-garden, whose roses have remained thornless ever since the saint threw himself into them as a means of overcoming diabolical temptations, stands a bronze statue of Saint Francis and the lamb by Rosignoli, which recalls the following story of Saint Bona-ventura :

'Not far from Santa Maria of the Portiuncola a lamb was once offered to the saint, and he accepted it gladly for its simplicity and innocence. He admonished the lamb that it must always be intent on praising God, and must carefully avoid doing harm to the brothers. And as though it knew the piety of the man of God, the lamb fully obeyed his commands. When it heard the brothers singing in choir, it hastened into the church, and without any teaching, it knelt down and bleated before the altar of the Virgin as though it too wished to praise her. And at the eleva-tion of the Blessed Sacrament it knelt as though, humble beast that it was, it desired to reprove the impious, and to encourage the pious to revere the most holy Sacrament.' [5]

Around the base of the statue of Saint Francis and the lamb

[5] Leg. Major, c. 8.

are four bas-reliefs recalling the incidents of Saint Francis and the cicala, Saint Francis and the crow, Saint Francis and the nightingale, and Saint Francis on his death-bed with the larks. In the basilica of Saint Francis, where 'no honour was too great for this Little Poor Man' and where 'people remembered his love, and wished to give back to him all he had left for their sakes,' the incomparable beauty of Giotto's fresco keeps alive the traditions of Saint Francis preaching to the birds. Gubbio will always be associated with the reconciliation which Saint Francis effected between the hungry wolf and the townspeople, while La Verna preserves the memory of the falcon who daily awakened the saint at an early hour to begin his prayers. That the love of Saint Francis extended to all creatures is well known from his inimitable 'Canticle of the Sun' which he wrote in the garden of the Sisters of Saint Clare at Saint Damian's, when he was severely ill and weighed down by many sorrows. The following rendering is that given in Fr. Cuthbert's *Life,* and includes the verse which the saint added when he made peace between the citizens of Assisi and the bishop, and the final verse that he added as he felt the approach of Sister Death :

Most high omnipotent good Lord,
  Thine are praise, glory and honour and all benediction,
To thee, alone, Most High, do they belong:
  And no man is there, worthy thee to name.

Praise be to thee, my Lord, with all thy creatures,
  Chiefest of all, Sir Brother Sun,
Who is our day, through whom thou givest light;
  Beautiful is he; radiant, with great splendour:
Of thee, Most High, he is a true revealer.

Praise be to thee, my Lord, for Sister Moon and for the stars;
  In heaven hast thou formed them, bright, precious and
    fair.

*Praise be to thee, my Lord, for Brother Wind, and for the
    air and for the cloud, for clear sky and all weathers,
By which thou givest nourishment to all thy creatures.*

*Praise be to thee, my Lord, for Sister Water; she
    Most useful is, and humble, precious and pure.*

*Praise be to thee, my Lord, for Brother Fire; by whom
    Thou lightest up the night;
And fair is he and merry, mighty and strong.*

*Praise be to thee, my Lord, for our Sister, Mother Earth,
    The which sustains and keeps us:
She brings forth divers fruits,
    The many-hued flowers and grass.*

*Praise be to thee, my Lord, for those who pardon grant for
    love of thee,
And weakness bear and buffetings;*

*Blessed are they who in peace abide,
For by thee, Most High, they shall be crowned.*

*Praise be to thee, my Lord, for our Sister, Bodily Death,
    from whom no living man can flee;
Woe is to them who die in mortal sin.
But blessed they who shall find themselves in thy most holy
    will:*

To them the second death shall do no ill.

*O creatures all, praise and bless my Lord and grateful be
    And serve him with deep humility.*

Saint Francis's love for all created things stemmed not from
any pantheistic tendencies but from a simple trust in Divine
Providence and from the conviction that all God's creatures share
a common Father. Not only did all created things fall under the
spell of Saint Francis's mysterious charm, but as Dom Vanden-

broucke has happily expressed it, 'the sanctity of Francis restored in some measure the atmosphere of the earthly paradise in which man lived in friendship with nature.' [6] But Saint Francis also loved the beauty of the world and he certainly lived in an outstandingly beautiful part of it. It is not to be wondered at that many of the places associated with the saint's deepest and most ecstatic spiritual experiences are near the summits of mountains, the Carceri, Grecchio, and La Verna, to take three outstanding examples. The modern pilgrim who makes the ascent of some 2,500 feet up the slopes of Mount Subasio and looks with veneration upon the grottoes used by the saint and his first companions, still visible on the steep, wooded hill-side, cannot but be deeply moved by the solitude, the beauty of the place and the primitive Franciscan simplicity, which still pervades the small fifteenth century Friary of Saint Bernardine of Siena; and he can understand why, as Celano tells us, Saint Francis 'loved to escape from the company of men, and to retire to remote places where, having put aside all anxious care and thought for others, he could live, only separated from his God by the veil of the flesh.' [7]

Saint Francis's way of life was no escapism, however. Like any one who has felt the call of God to enter into union with himself and who has at the same time responded to the commission of the Gospel to go into the world and teach all nations, Saint Francis felt the tension between the claims of the active and the contemplative life most keenly. On one occasion he had become so tormented by the question as to whether he should go on with his preaching tours or whether he should betake himself to some hermitage and spend the rest of his life in prayer and contemplation, that he decided to seek the advice of two of his followers whom he could trust, Saint Clare and Brother Silvester, and sent Brother Masseo to enquire of them. The *Fioretti* records that when Brother Masseo returned, 'Saint Francis received him with

[6] op. cit., p. 354.
[7] Leg. 1, c. 6.

the greatest charity, washed his feet, and prepared his repast. And after he had eaten Saint Francis called him into the wood, and kneeling before him, he let down his hood, and stretching out his arms in the form of the cross, he asked, "What does my Lord Jesus Christ command that I should do?" And Brother Masseo answered, "As to Brother Silvester, so to Sister Clare, with her sisters, has Christ answered and revealed that his will is that thou shouldest go into the world to preach, because he has not elected thee for thyself alone, but also for the salvation of others." Then Saint Francis, having heard this reply and knowing by this what was the will of Jesus Christ, arose with great fervour and said, "Let us go in the name of God." ' [8]

Not long after this Saint Francis went out to preach the words of Christ and to set an example of Christian living not only in Europe but in the Moslem lands of the East, where he finally came into contact with Melek-el-Kamil, Sultan of Egypt and leader of the Saracen hosts. It is well-known how Saint Francis went fearlessly into the camp of the Sultan, and, although he made friends with him, failed to convert him. Wherever he was and whatever his mission, whether engaged on preaching tours or whether consulting cardinals and popes concerning the welfare of his Order, Saint Francis's activities were marked by a singular love for the Church and by an outstanding zeal for her truth and holiness. The humility and loyalty of Saint Francis is seen in the fact that he forbade the friars to preach in any parish before they had received the permission of the parish priest, and not to preach at all in any diocese where the bishop of the diocese had opposed their preaching. 'Know, my Brethren,' Saint Francis once said in a 'conference' delivered to his brethren, 'that the salvation of souls is most pleasing to God, and this we shall procure much better by living in concord with the clergy than by being at variance with them. If they hinder this work, God is their judge, and he will avenge it in due time. Therefore be subject to the Prelates, that, as far as you can prevent it, no envy

[8] Ch. 15.

may arise. If you are the sons of peace, you will gain both the clergy and the people, and this will be much more acceptable to God than if you gained the people only, and scandalized the clergy. Hide their faults, supply their deficiencies; and when you have done this, humble yourselves all the more.' [9]

Next to love in Saint Paul's enumeration of the fruits of the Spirit is joy, and joy was one of the most characteristic marks of the spiritual life of Saint Francis. Not that he was ever hilarious or flippant. His joy stemmed from a sense of gratitude for all that God is and for all his gifts in creation and redemption. The second *Life* of Celano records that 'Saint Francis used to say that the most powerful remedy against the thousand snares and pit-falls of the devil was a joyful spirit. He declared: "The devil is delighted above all when he succeeds in robbing a servant of God of his joy of spirit. . . . When the devils see a servant of Christ filled with holy joy, they cannot harm him; but if he is tearful, bitter, depressed and gloomy, it may come about that he will either remain wrapped in self-pity or turn to empty distractions." The saint therefore strove to live constantly with a cheerful heart, and to keep his soul burning brightly with the oil of joy.' [10]

Yet the saint often wept. Not on his own account, but on account of the sufferings of Christ and of men's indifference to them and to the outpoured love of God. It is said that from the time the crucifix in Saint Damian's 'spoke' to him he could never think of the Passion of his Master without weeping, and it is not surprising that the popular devotion of the Stations of the Cross is associated with the name of Saint Francis. In the friary at Grecchio, there is a deeply moving picture of the saint weeping over the rejection of Christ in the hearts of so many, lamenting that Love is not loved. It was at Grecchio, also, that Saint Francis first set up the Christmas crib, in an age which in respect of its forgetfulness was so strikingly like our own, to recall men to the true meaning of Christmas. 'I want to show,' he said, 'that Babe

[9] *Works*, p. 115.
[10] II Cel. II, 88.

of Bethlehem in such a way that we may see with our bodily eyes all that he suffered through lack of what is needful to a new-born Child, how he was placed in a manger, and lay on hay between the ox and ass.' [11]

At the beginning of this chapter it was pointed out that Saint Francis can only be understood when he is thought of pre-eminently as one who wished to follow our Lord even to the drinking of the cup of his Passion. He not only felt compassion for the sufferings of Christ, but he longed for the privilege of being identified with his Lord in his sufferings. The saint's whole life of witness, service, sacrifice and suffering may be thought of as a whole unified act of reparation for the sins of mankind which put Christ on the Cross, for his own sins and the sins of the Church, and for the sins of indifference and rejection of his contemporaries. In 1224, on Holy Cross Day itself, the saint had been praying on Mount La Verna which Count Orlando da Chiusi had given to him as a place of retreat as far back as 1213, and which still carries the spirit of what happened there on this never-to-be-forgotten day. The saint's prayer, that he might feel in his body and soul the sufferings of the Crucified and might feel also the love of Jesus that enabled him to endure such agony on behalf of sinners, was answered in a most remarkable way. Brother Leo observed the saint wrapped in an ecstasy of joy and wonder, after which his body bore wounds in his hands and feet and side, like those of the Crucified Christ, wounds which caused him pain until the day of his death and which, despite all his efforts to conceal them, became known to many. What exactly happened we shall never know, but a full account of the miracle is given both in the *Fioretti* and in the first of Celano's *Lives*. Before they left La Verna the saint wrote on a piece of parchment his simple blessing of Brother Leo, which the latter carried next to his heart until the day of his death. It can still be seen in the sacristy of the Church of Saint Francis at Assisi, still showing

[11] I Cel. 30.

E

the saint's autograph and the creases where Brother Leo folded it up.

Until the day of his death Saint Francis was never free from illness and pain, which he bore with his characteristic gentleness, humility and joy. He spent the last days of his life at his beloved Portiuncola. When death was approaching he asked to be laid on the bare ground, and having composed the final verse of his 'Canticle of the Sun,' Celano tells us that 'while all the brothers of whom he was the father and the guide were gathered there reverently awaiting his blessed transitus and end, that most holy soul left the flesh to be absorbed into the abyss of eternal light, while his body fell asleep in the Lord.' [12] That was on October 3rd, 1226. Two years later he was canonized and immediately after the work on the great basilica of Saint Francis at Assisi, which now holds his tomb, was begun. It may not be difficult to agree with Clémenceau that 'the only remedy for our present corruption is that every Christian should have in his veins one drop of the blood of the Little Poor Man of Assisi.' In any case, the collect for the Feast of the Stigmata of Saint Francis of Assisi (September 17th) expresses the need of the contemporary world for the message of Saint Francis, which is the message of the Gospel :

'O Lord Jesus Christ, Who, when the world was growing cold, in order to inflame our hearts with the fire of Thy love, didst renew in the body of the most blessed Francis the sacred marks of Thy Passion; Graciously grant that, through his merits and prayers, we may ever bear Thy Cross, and bring forth fruits worthy of repentance; Who livest and reignest with the Father and the Holy Spirit, one God, world without end. Amen.'

[12] Cel. 8.

CHAPTER 4

RAMON LULL
c. 1235–1315

IN studying the lives and writings of the masters of the spiritual
life across the countries and down the centuries, one is frequently
made aware of their fundamental, common humanity; and not
least in respect of the temptations to which they were a prey.
From some points of view, perhaps, it is as comforting as it is
usually astonishing to those whose feet are as yet on the lower
rungs of what Walter Hilton called the Ladder of Perfection, to
realize that one of the severest and most recurrent temptations
besetting those who persevere on their Godward way is the
temptation to dejection and despondency. On one such occasion,
Saint Francis of Assisi was encouraged to persevere when he had
a vision of the future, assuring him of the growth of his Order:
'I have seen a great host of men coming to us,' he told his
brethren, 'and desiring to live with us in this habit and holy life
under the Rule of this blessed Order. In my ears there is still the
sound of their coming and going at the command of holy
obedience. I have seemed to see the roads thronged by a great
host of men assembling in these parts out of nearly every nation.
The French are coming, Spaniards hurrying, Germans and English running, and a vast company from many other races are
hastening towards us.' [1]

The embracing of the Franciscan way of life was not to be
confined, however, to the first Order of the Friars Minor, nor to
the Sisters of Saint Clare. So great was the appeal of the Franciscan ideal to men and women in all walks of life that in 1221
Saint Francis made provision for their needs and aspirations by
founding the Third Order. The members of it, Tertiaries as they
were and are called, were pledged to simplicity of life, to engage

[1] I Celano 11.

in prayer and work on behalf of the needy, and to further the salvation of souls by all means in their power, while at the same time carrying on their avocations in the world. The idea grew so widely that to this day most religious Orders both under the Roman and the Anglican Obedience support, and are supported by, a Third Order or similar association, which is motivated by the same ideals and aims as the Order or Community itself. In the thirteenth century, one of the greatest of Franciscan tertiaries was the Catalan poet and missionary, Ramon Lull.

Ramon Lull was born at Majorca, where his father, having accompanied King James of Catalonia-Aragon on the expedition in which he captured Majorca from the Moors, had bought a quantity of land and had decided to settle down there, with the evident intention of founding one of the leading Majorcan families of the future. The education and leisure pursuits of young Ramon were such as would fit him for the life of a courtier. At the age of fourteen he became a page at the court of King James, where he established a firm friendship with the two royal princes, Peter and James.

In 1256 Ramon accompanied Prince James, whom his father intimated would become king of Majorca in due course, first on a visit to his future realm and then through most of Spain and part of France. Lull was sociable and easy-going, as well as elegant and gay. He lived at the time when the art of the troubadour was at its height, and neither his marriage nor the subsequent birth of his son and daughter reduced his susceptibility to the attractions of beautiful women, whose charms he celebrated in songs which gave his poetic gifts ample scope.

Lull was already thirty years old when he had a vivid experience, reminiscent of that of Saint Francis before the crucifix in Saint Damian's, which changed the course and character of the whole of the rest of his life. As he sat humming the tune and composing the words of his latest love-song, he became vividly aware of Someone gazing at him, the Someone being, as a Catalan biography of Lull written during his lifetime described the vision, 'our Lord Jesus Christ hanging upon the Cross,' bearing an expression of 'great agony and sorrow.' Four times more the astonished and frightened young man had the same experience as he strove to complete his song. As his disturbed emotions gave way before reasoned reflection he became convinced that these appearances of the Crucified were objective visions, and that the meaning of them was, as the contemporary biography records, that 'Our Lord God Jesus desired none other thing than that he should wholly abandon the world and devote himself to his service.' [2]

Like many another who has responded wholeheartedly to the call of God only after many years of a self-seeking and pleasure-filled life, he was overcome with deep penitence for his past life and with an anxious questioning as to whether, in view of his misspent years, what was left of his life could be offered to God. Like Saint Francis, again, he became vividly aware of some words of the Gospel speaking to him with special intensity : 'Greater love hath no man than this, that a man lay down his life for his friends.' Thus he aspired to no less a sacrifice. But not without counting the cost. He set apart part of his wealth for the support of his wife and children and, having sold the remainder, he gave the proceeds to the poor. He then broke with his former life by leaving Majorca and going on pilgrimage for a year or more, which included a visit to Santiago de Compostela, the city of Saint James, the patron of Spain.

On his return he set himself to put into effect the three resolves which he had made immediately after his conversion, namely, to write books on apologetics, to work for the provision of missionary colleges, and to lay down his life as a martyr. To the furtherance of these three objectives he dedicated the whole of the rest of his long and active, yet contemplative, life. The greatest challenge to Christianity in Lull's day came, as in many parts of the world to-day, from Islam. In order to confront the Muslim world with the message of the Gospel Lull realized that he must not

[2] Quoted E. A. Peers, *Fool of Love,* S.C.M. Press, 1946, p. 13.

only learn Arabic but make himself a master of Arabic studies. Having abandoned his original intention of studying in Paris, Lull settled in Palma, which still included many Moors and where he was already well-known. Knowing nothing of more positive and more pacific methods of missionary technique, which are psychologically adjusted to the modern temper without being necessarily syncretistic, Ramon Lull testified both to the Franciscan spirit which inspired his devotion as well as to the reality of his conversion when, despite the derision he encountered in the streets, he went about dressed in a habit of the coarsest cloth he could find and, especially in later years, did not hesitate to offer frontal attacks in public on the beliefs of the Muslims. Men thought him a fool, but he was learning the compensations that can only be enjoyed as the fruit of entire self-surrender. 'I am clothed in vile raiment; but love clothes my heart with thoughts of delight, and my body with tears, griefs and sufferings.' [3] He who had once found pleasure and skill in the art of the troubadour now found his whole delight in giving his life to the praise of the divine love; indeed, the title he most liked to give himself was the 'Fool of Love.'

During the next nine years which he spent in study, from 1266–75, he also wrote a great deal. His first book, the *Book of the Gentile and the Three Wise Men,* although largely unconvincing from the psychological, religious and literary aspects, especially from the modern standpoint, is nevertheless important because it was his first of a type of writing in which Lull loved to engage, that of the religious allegory. His purpose in writing it was apologetic as can be seen from his reference to it in the *Book of the Lover and the Beloved:* ' "Say, O Fool! Wherein hast thou knowledge that the Catholic Faith is true, and that the beliefs of the Jews and Saracens are falsehood and error?" He answered : "In the ten conditions of the *Book of the Gentile and the Three Wise Men.*" ' [4]

[3] *Book of the Lover and the Beloved.* Tr. Peers, S.P.C.K., no. 149.
[4] ibid., no. 287.

The same apologetic purpose inspired his enormous work, *The Book of Contemplation,* which occupied him for nearly twelve months, which he first wrote in Arabic before translating it. Its present Catalan edition occupies seven volumes involving about one million words. In Lull's use of the word 'contemplation' the book was meant to be a method of meditation or serious thought for daily use 'by men learned and men simple, secular and religious, rich and poor.' [5] The book gives many a vivid picture of contemporary society and ranges across many subjects, but its significance in the spiritual life of its author can be seen in the following observation of the late Professor Peers : 'Among the semi-autobiographical themes of the *Book of Contemplation* one stands high above the rest : the conversion of unbelievers. This book alone establishes that it was the ruling passion of his life.' [6]

It may seem a remarkable thing that Ramon Lull spent so long a time in study and writing when he was no longer young, and when he longed to venture forth to Moslem lands and spend his amazing energy in a life of evangelization. That he lost neither his enthusiasm for active missionary work nor his desire to die a martyr's death during this protracted period of preparation for his life's work he himself revealed, when he had completed about one-third of his *Book of Contemplation:* 'So great desire has Thy servant to give Thee praise, that by day and by night he toils and struggles as best he may to bring to an end this *Book of Contemplation;* and then, when once it is completed, he will go and shed both blood and tears for Thee in the Holy Land wherein Thou didst shed Thy precious blood. . . . Till this book be ended, Thy servant and lover may not go to the land of the Saracens to give praise to Thy glorious name. . . . Wherefore I pray Thee to aid Thy servant . . . that he may speedily go and suffer martyrdom for Thy love, if it be Thy will that he may be found worthy thereof.' [7]

[5] *Fool of Love,* p. 25.
[6] ibid., p. 28.
[7] ibid., p. 51.

Only the briefest mention can be made of the long train of events which finally brought him to his desired goal, if adequate attention is to be devoted to his writings. From the time when he completed his studies in Palma in 1275, when he was already forty-two, until, 'unwearying and unwearied,' he died a martyr's death at Bugia in 1315 at the ripe old age of eighty-two, his time was spent in many journeys; on numerous visits to Paris and other centres of learning to dispute the doctrines of the Averroists or to expound the theology underlying his major work, the *Ars Magna;* or to Rome to press before successive popes his schemes for the provision of missionary colleges so that those engaged in apologetics with the Moslem world in particular might have a thorough grounding in theology and languages; and in writing an enormous profusion of books. Yet the foundation-stone of all this almost feverish activity was a life of prayer in which this devoted and dedicated layman had already attained a high degree of union with God.

Through his life and writings Ramon Lull is revealed as a theologian and as a poet as well as a missionary and evangelist. Towards the end of his long stay at Palma he wrote his famous *Ars Magna,* a theological treatise which was approved by the University of Paris—a fact which caused Ramon frequently to refer to himself as Master Lull. It made a great appeal at the time when the conflict roused by the teaching of the Averroists was raging fiercely, and especially in Paris. By identifying philosophical and theological truth—in a way which caused Gregory XI to condemn his teaching in 1376 but which was in open contrast to the Averroists who completely separated them—Master Lull attempted to work out a method whereby all questions of theology, metaphysics and even natural science could be answered, and whereby all possible knowledge could be reduced to, or derived from, first principles. Such was his 'ars' or method, and some twenty years later, Lull was still crusading against the Averroists with their denial of personal immortality, of freedom of the will and of moral responsibility, when he wrote the *Tree of the Philo-*

sophy of Love, which Professor Peers describes 'as delightful and profitable a book to dip into as Ramon ever wrote. It moves in various and varied mediums—in maxim and allegory, subtlety and simplicity, poetry and prose, exposition, meditation and prayer. Never for long is it devoid of grace and charm, nor of the fervour of a single-minded lover of beauty, wholly devoted to God. Though not a mystical treatise, it abounds in the raw material of all mysticism—an unquenchable desire.' [8]

The present-day reader of Ramon Lull will most likely derive more profit and delight from the patriarch of Catalan literature than from the crusader against Averroist doctrines. This being so, most will regard *Blanquerna* as his masterpiece. *Blanquerna* is a religious romance in which 'the reasoner is succeeded by the dreamer, the mystic and the poet.' [9] Blanquerna, the hero, is the only, idolized son of elderly, devout and wealthy parents, who intend that when he comes of age, they shall embrace the Religious life, leaving their possessions and the management of their estates to him. To their great dismay they discover that Blanquerna is intent upon leading a hermit life, and when their schemes to deflect him from his course fail, he leaves home and they sell their estates, endow a hospital, and, waiting upon the patients themselves, live from day to day, as the friars did, 'begging for the love of God.' The rest of the book describes Blanquerna's wanderings in one of Lull's typical forests, 'through the strangeness and solitariness of (which) place, and the heavens and the stars, his soul was highly exalted in the contemplation of God'[10]; and his many adventures until he eventually becomes Pope, although he has never forgotten 'the desire which he had aforetime to lead the life of a hermit,'[11] and which he finally attains. Eventually, he takes up his abode 'upon a high mountain wherein was the church of a hermitage, near to a fountain.' [12]

[8] *Fool of Love,* p. 78.
[9] ibid., p. 42.
[10] *Blanquerna.* Tr. Peers, 1926, p. 155.
[11] ibid., p. 402.
[12] ibid., p. 404.

Many examples could be taken to illustrate the poetical and contemplative quality of Ramon Lull's writing and the greatness of his literary achievement but one must suffice, namely, the passage in which Blanquerna's mother laments to the Virgin Mother of God over her son's departure:

'I have had but one son and he it is whom thy Son takes from me. In peril of evil men and of wild beasts he makes him to go; alone he will make him to be all the days of his life; raw herbs he will eat; his clothing will be but his skin, and his locks, and the air around him. Do thou look down and see how fair is my son Blanquerna in his person and in his mind; think thou how sun and wind and nakedness will darken him and destroy the beauty of his features. When he is cold, who will give him warmth? when he is sick, who will tend him? When he hungers, who will give him to eat? If he fears, who will strengthen him? If thou aidest not my son, even without my prayers, where would be thy pity and thy mercy? Let the grief that I have for my son, as I behold him going to his death, in affliction and penance, alone in the forest, I know not whither, call to mind the grief that thou hadst for thy Son when thou sawest him done to death and crucified.' [13]

After the hermit's departure there follow two opuscules, the *Book of the Lover and the Beloved* and the *Art of Contemplation,* which are supposed to have been written by the hermit. The *Book of the Lover and the Beloved* is obviously autobiographical and the fruit of Lull's own contemplation, undoubtedly on Mount Randa, 'the mount of the Beloved,' towering above Palma Bay, and at other times as well. Indeed, it is this book, above all else, which entitles its author to figure among the masters of the spiritual life and to be ranked as a forerunner of the great Spanish mystics, Saint Theresa and Saint John of the Cross. In the oldest extant catalogue of Lull's writings, the *Book of the Lover and the Beloved* appears independently of *Blanquerna* and it is invariably printed separately in modern times. It is unmis-

[13] *Blanquerna,* p. 74.

takably complete in itself and 'represents the climax, not only of the romance but, according to present-day ideas, of the whole of Lull's writing. Since Lullian studies have taken renewed life and a more modern orientation, it has come to be regarded as the centre-piece of his work, as the book which points to the source of his inspiration and as the earnest of his literary immortality.' [14]

Many who wish to use the *Book of the Lover and the Beloved* as an aid to their own devotion will find a practical convenience in the fact that there are as many verses as days in the year, and may well come to echo the belief that 'while a spark of love for God remains in a human soul, it is unthinkable that Ramon's sublime hymns of love can ever perish.' [15]

To any one more familiar with the theology of the New Testament, and especially that of Saint Paul and Saint John where God appears as the Divine Lover, than with the language of medieval mysticism, a word of explanation may be helpful. In a previous chapter mention has been made of the devotion to the humanity of Christ which characterized much of the writings of Saint Bernard. This devotion persisted and grew during the Middle Ages and appears to have had a large influence on the language of Christian spirituality, so that Ramon Lull, for example, finds it natural to speak of the human soul as the Lover and of God, Father, Son, Creator and Redeemer, as the Beloved. For example,

'They asked the Lover : "Who is thy Beloved?" He answered : "He that makes me to love, desire, faint, sigh, weep, endure reproaches and die." ' [16]

'They asked the Beloved : "Who is Thy Lover?" He answered : "He that shrinks from naught so that he may honour and praise My Name, and renounces all things to obey My commandments and counsels." ' [17] As well as the clearly defined figures of the Lover and the Beloved there is also the shadowy, allegorical figure of Love, who plays a part often not unlike the almost personified

[14] *Fool of Love,* p. 47.
[15] ibid., p. 121.
[16] *Book of the Lover and the Beloved,* no. 237.
[17] ibid., no. 238.

Wisdom of Israel's Wisdom literature, being sometimes the Lover's close companion, sometimes a more transcendent personality endowing the Lover with noble gifts, and always an essential element in the communication of the Lover with the Beloved. For example,

'Far above Love is the Beloved; far beneath it is the Lover; and love, which lies between these two, makes the Beloved to descend to the Lover, and the Lover to rise toward the Beloved. And this ascending and descending are the beginning and the life of that love whereby the Lover suffers and the Beloved is served.'

'On the right side of Love stands the Beloved, and on the left side is the Lover; and thus he cannot reach the Beloved unless he pass through Love.' [18]

Like the Little Poor Man of Assisi, the Fool of Love longed to make reparation to his Beloved for the wrongs, insults and slights that he suffered at the hands of men, and many of the aspirations in the *Book of the Lover and the Beloved* express this longing. For example,

'The Lover met his Beloved, and saw Him to be very noble and powerful and worthy of all honour. And he cried : "How strange a thing it is that so few among men know and love and honour Thee as Thou deservest!" And the Beloved answered him and said : "Greatly has man grieved Me; for I created him to know Me, love Me, and honour Me, and yet, of every thousand, but a hundred fear and love Me; and ninety of these fear Me lest I should condemn them to Hell, and ten love Me that I may grant them Glory; hardly is there one who loves Me for My goodness and nobility." When the Lover heard these words, he wept bitterly for the dishonour paid to his Beloved; and he said : "Ah, Beloved, how much hast Thou given to man and how greatly hast Thou honoured him! Why then has man thus forgotten Thee?" . . . The Beloved said to His Lover : "Thou shalt praise and defend Me in those places where men most fear to praise Me." ' [19]

18 *Book of the Lover and the Beloved,* nos. 258 and 259.
19 ibid., nos. 218 and 315.

The whole motive of Lull's own apostolate and the reflection of his experiences can be seen shining through many of the colloquies between the Lover and the Beloved, for example :

'They asked the Lover : "Wilt thou sell thy desire?" He answered : "I have sold it already to my Beloved, for such a price as would buy the whole world."

' "Preach thou, O Fool, and speak concerning thy Beloved; weep and fast." So the Lover renounced the world, and went forth with love to seek his Beloved, and praise Him in those places wherein He was dishonoured.' [20]

The extent to which external works may be united with contemplative activity in the soul of one whose life is set upon the unitive way, and is already hid with Christ in God, is glimpsed in the following passage :

'The heart of the Lover soared to the heights of the Beloved, so that he might not be impeded from loving Him in the abyss of this world. And when he reached his Beloved he contemplated Him with sweetness and delight. But the Beloved led him down again to this world that he might contemplate him in tribulations and griefs.' [21] The *Book of the Lover and the Beloved* depicts the lover as one whose only desire and whose ultimate goal is to be one with the Beloved. 'Said the Lover to his Beloved : "Thou art all, and through all, and in all, and with all. I will have Thee wholly that I may have and be myself wholly." The Beloved answered : "Thou canst not have Me wholly unless thou art Mine." And the Lover said : "Let me be wholly Thine and be Thou wholly mine." ' [22] The *Book of the Lover and the Beloved* is no systematic treatise as to how the life of Union, or the Unitive way, is to be reached, but it is clear that in the spiritual awakening and progress of the Lover the Purgative and the Illuminative ways both have their parts to play : 'Long and perilous are the paths whereby the Lover seeks his Beloved. They

[20] *Book of the Lover and the Beloved,* nos. 280 and 281.
[21] ibid., no. 56.
[22] ibid., no. 68.

77

are peopled by considerations, sighs and tears. They are lit up by love.' [23] The book abounds in references to the sufferings and penances of the Lover, the purpose and the effect of which is to bring him nearer to his Beloved :

'Sins and merits were striving among themselves in the conscience and the will of the Lover. Justice and remembrance increased his consciousness of sin, but mercy and hope increased the assurance of pardon in the will of the Beloved; wherefore in the penitence of the Lover merits conquered sins and wrongs.' [24]

The insights of the Illuminative way enable the Lover to declare :

'They asked the Lover : "What is the greatest darkness?" He answered : "The absence of my Beloved." "And what is the greatest light?" "The presence of my Beloved." ' [25]

It is the Beloved himself who 'illumines faith and kindles devotion,' and faith and devotion are a 'ladder whereby understanding may rise to a comprehension of the secrets' [26] of the Beloved.

When a soul is set upon the way of union even temptations are a means of bringing the soul nearer to God :

'The Lover made complaint to his Beloved concerning the temptations which came to him daily to afflict his thoughts. And the Beloved made answer, saying that temptations are an occasion whereby man may have recourse to memory, making remembrance of God and loving His honours and perfections.' [27]

There are many verses in which Lull treats of the place of the memory, the understanding and the will in the spiritual life. Their interrelation is brought out in the following verse :

'As one that was a fool went the Lover through a city, singing of his Beloved; and men asked him if he had lost his wits. "My Beloved," he answered, "has taken my will, and I myself have

[23] *Book of the Lover and the Beloved,* no. 2.
[24] ibid., no. 204.
[25] ibid., no. 124.
[26] ibid., no. 288.
[27] ibid., no. 343.

yielded up to Him my understanding; so that there is left in me naught but memory, wherewith I remember my Beloved." ' [28]

The *Book of the Lover and the Beloved* abounds in examples of the prayers of the Lover, which are short and vivid, such as, 'Thou that fillest the sun with splendour, fill my heart with love'; and with his aspirations and considerations, which are often expressed in forceful metaphors or short parables, as, for example, the following:

'The keys of the doors of love are gilded with meditations, sighs and tears; the cord which binds them is woven of conscience, contrition, devotion and satisfaction; the door is kept by justice and mercy.

'The Lover beat upon the door of his Beloved with blows of love and hope. The Beloved heard the blows of His Lover, with humility, pity, charity and patience. Deity and Humanity opened the doors, and the Lover went in to his Beloved.' [29]

Within the pages of the *Book of the Lover and the Beloved* one catches the echo of the desire for martyrdom which never left that passionately devoted missionary, Lull himself, in the fifty years of his single-minded apostolate. For example, 'Ah! When shall the Lover with joy lay down his life for the Beloved?' [30] Or again, it is surely of martyrdom that he is thinking when he writes, 'So the Lover desired to wear crimson garments daily, that his dress might be more like to the dress of his Beloved.' [31] At last, however, the veteran evangelist had his wish granted. As he boldly proclaimed the truth of the Gospel to which he had devoted his life, an angry crowd began to stone him. Whether he died immediately or in the ship that carried him back to his native land is not known for certain, but one can feel that the words of his own book might have been written about himself: 'The Beloved revealed Himself to His Lover, clothed in new and scarlet

[28] *Book of the Lover and the Beloved,* no. 54.
[29] ibid., nos. 42, 43.
[30] ibid., no. 5.
[31] ibid., no. 262.

robes. He stretched out His Arms to embrace him; He inclined His Head to kiss him.' [32] His body was finally interred by the Franciscans in their friary, and the people of Majorca still venerate him as a blessed, though uncanonized, saint. In 1915, at the sexcentenary of his death, his remains were re-enclosed in a coffin of cedar wood. No more appropriate words can be found to end this chapter than those which are engraved upon that coffin, words which, in their turn, form part of the epitaph of the lover from one of Lull's own books, the *Tree of Love*.

'Here lies a Lover, who has died for his Beloved, and for love . . ., who has loved his Beloved with a love that is good, great and enduring . . ., who has battled bravely for love's sake . . ., who has striven against false love and false lovers . . ., a Lover ever humble, patient, loyal, ardent, liberal, prudent, holy and full of all good things, inspiring many lovers to honour and serve his Beloved.' [33]

[32] *Book of the Lover and the Beloved*, no. 91.
[33] *Fool of Love*, pp. 105–6.

CHAPTER 5

JAN VAN RUYSBROECK
1293–1381

In the judgment of no lesser authority than the late Evelyn Underhill 'Jan van Ruysbroeck is the greatest of the Flemish mystics, and must take high rank in any list of Christian contemplatives and saints.' In any study of the spirituality of the Old Testament, the New Testament or of nearly two thousand years of Christian history one cannot fail to notice the wide diversity of gifts and temperaments, of occupations and circumstances among those whom God calls to his service and who respond with a complete oblation of themselves to his will and purpose. While Jan van Ruysbroeck shares with the other masters of the spiritual life so far studied the distinction of offering the all of man in return for the all of God, he is notably different from them in a number of striking ways. Unlike Saint Benedict, he did not have to turn violently against the grain of his own temperament and natural inclinations; unlike Saint Bernard, he did not have to turn his back on a life rank and secular importance; unlike Saint Francis, he did not, apparently, have to have all his ideals shattered before he could refashion them according to the pattern of God's remaking; unlike Ramon Lull, he had no gay and mis-spent youth of which to repent. Whereas Saint Bernard, Saint Francis and Ramon Lull lived out their contemplative vocation, as did the Apostle Paul, 'in journeyings oft,' van Ruysbroeck spent his whole life within his native province of Brabant.

Jan van Ruysbroeck was born in 1293 at a small village between Brussels and Hal which bears the same name as himself. It appears that at the age of eleven he ran away from home to escape from the excessive affection and solicitude of his mother. He found his way to Brussels to the house of a relative, Jan Hinckaert, who was a Canon of Saint Gudule in Brussels, and

F

who took the lad in, gave him a home and educated him. He had notable ability as a theologian, although he had no enthusiasm for the disputations of the schoolmen. In 1317, he was ordained to the priesthood, and having obtained a prebend's stall in Saint Gudule, he remained there for twenty-six years fulfilling the ordinary duties of his priesthood within the context of a contemplative vocation. The biographer of van Ruysbroeck does not find himself recording or interpreting a series of dramatic or epoch-making events, yet while van Ruysbroeck was carrying out his cathedral duties he was also finding out in personal experience the deep realities of the spiritual life which he expounded so beautifully and movingly in his writings. He was finding out, for example, one of the most important secrets of the interior life of the Christian, namely that of meeting with Christ in the ordinary circumstances of everyday life, what he called 'the second coming of Christ.' Using the familiar and beloved image of Christ as the Bridegroom of the soul, he writes of it thus in the *Adornment of the Spiritual Marriage:*

'The second coming of Christ our Bridegroom takes place every day within good men; often and many times, with new graces and gifts, in all who make themselves ready for it, each according to his power. We would not speak here of a man's first conversion, nor of the first grace that was given to him when he turned from sin to the virtues. But we would speak of an increase of new gifts and new virtues from day to day, and of the present coming of Christ our Bride-groom which takes place daily within our souls. . . .

'Now understand this : when the sun sends its beams and its radiance into a deep valley between two high mountains, and, standing in the zenith, can yet shine upon the bottom and ground of the valley, then three things happen : the valley becomes full of light by reflection from the mountains, and it receives more heat, and becomes more fruitful than the plain and level country. And so likewise, when a good man takes his stand upon his own littleness, in the most lowly part of himself, and confesses and knows that he has nothing, and is nothing and can do nothing, of himself, neither stand still nor go on, and when he sees how often he fails in virtues and good works : then he confesses his poverty and his helplessness, then he makes a valley of humility. And when he is thus humble and needy, and knows his own need, he lays his distress, and complains of it, before the bounty and the mercy of God. And so he marks the sublimity of God and his own lowliness; and thus he becomes a deep valley. And Christ is a Sun of righteousness and also of mercy, who stands in the highest part of the firmament, that is, on the right hand of the Father, and thence he shines into the bottom of the humble heart; for Christ is always moved by helplessness, whenever a man complains of it and lays it before him with humility. Then there arise two mountains, that is, two desires; one to serve God and praise him with reverence, the other to attain noble virtues. Those two mountains are higher than the heavens, for these longings touch God without intermediary, and crave his ungrudging generosity. And then that generosity cannot withhold itself, it must flow forth; for then the soul is made ready to receive, and to hold, more gifts.

'These are the wherefore, and the way of the new coming with new virtues. Then, this valley, the humble, radiant heart, receives three things : it becomes more radiant and enlightened by grace, it becomes more ardent in charity, and it becomes more fruitful in perfect virtues and in good works. And thus you have the why, the way, and the work of this coming.' [1]

For Ruysbroeck himself, there was no dichotomy, no false distinction, between the life of service and the life of worship, between ethics and religion, between the active and the contemplative aspects of the Christian apostolate. For him indeed they were twin peaks, as it were, in a life of adoration. It is evident that as he ministered year by year in the office of priesthood the 'mysterious working of Christ in the sacraments,' to use his own phrase, increasingly took possession of his life, and his

[1] *Adornment of the Spiritual Marriage,* Ch. vi.

writings reveal that he had a special devotion to our Lord in the Holy Sacrament of the Altar, which he calls 'a special treasure which Christ has left in Holy Church to all good men.' [2] However much he reached the heights of personal mystical experience, and however much he expounded and taught the art of contemplation to others, he never by-passed the covenanted means of grace nor minimized their importance, as can be seen, for example, in the chapter of the *Adornment of the Spiritual Marriage* entitled 'Showing how Christ has given himself to all in common in the Sacrament of the Altar.' When a man receives the Sacrament in a state of recollection and preparedness, 'then he shall go out to meet Christ in the same way in which Christ comes to meet him. He shall lift up himself to receive Christ with his heart, with his desire, with sensible love, with all his powers, and with a joyful craving.' During this our earthly pilgrimage the Sacrament of the Altar not only provides us with nourishment for our soul's need and redeems our common humanity by bringing us into contact with the Man, Jesus Christ, but it is the principal means whereby we begin here and now to enter upon that life of union with God, which is our inheritance and goal in eternity. Of the gift of the Body and Blood of Christ in the Sacrament Ruysbroeck writes : 'In this gift Christ gives himself to us in three ways. He gives us his Flesh and his Blood and his bodily life, glorified and full of joy and sweetness ; he gives us his spirit with its highest powers, full of glory and gifts, truth and righteousness ; and he gives us his personality through that Divine Light which raises his spirit and all enlightened spirits into the most high and fruitive unity.

'Now Christ desires that we shall remember him so often as we consecrate, offer and receive his Body. Consider now how we shall remember him. We shall mark and behold how Christ inclines himself towards us with loving affection, with great desire, and with yearning delight, and with a warm and tender outpouring of himself into our bodily nature. For he gives us that

[2] *Adornment,* Ch. vii.

which he has in common with our manhood, that is, his Flesh and his Blood, and his bodily nature. We shall also mark and behold that precious body martyred, pierced and wounded for our sake, because of his love and his faithfulness towards us. Herewith we are adorned and nourished in the lower part of our manhood. In this most high gift of the Sacrament he also gives us his spirit, full of glory and rich gifts of virtue, and unspeakable marvels of charity and nobleness. And herewith we are nourished and adorned and enlightened in the unity of our spirit and in the higher powers, through the indwelling of Christ with all his riches. Moreover he gives us in the Sacrament of the Altar his most high personality in incomprehensible splendour. And through this we are lifted up to and united with the Father, and the Father receives his adopted sons together with his natural Son, and thus we enter into our inheritance of the Godhead in eternal blessedness.' [3]

During the years of his faithful ministry as well as afterwards Jan van Ruysbroeck won among his contemporaries a reputation for kindness, gentleness, humility and meekness. During his later years as Prior of Groenendael he frequently reserved to himself the most humble and menial tasks. In winter, especially in snowy weather, he was wont to show particular solicitude for the birds, and was careful to see that they were fed. His beautiful description of meekness as one of the 'four daughters' of humility, which forms the fourth of his *Seven Steps of the Ladder of Spiritual Love,* is thoroughly in keeping with his character and may well appear to his commentators as a portrait of its author :

 ' "Blessed are the meek, for they shall possess the land," that is, their soul and body, in peace; for on the humble and meek rests the Spirit of the Lord. And when our spirit is lifted up and united to the Spirit of God, then we bear that yoke of Christ which is sweet and gentle, and we are laden with his burden which is light. For his love does not labour, and the more we love the lighter is our burden; for when we carry love, it carries

[3] *Adornment,* Ch. 47, pp. 112–13.

us above all the heavens to him whom we love. For the loving spirit flies whither it will; all the heavens are open to it, and it has its soul always in its hands and sends it where it will. It has found within itself the treasure of its soul, Christ, its dear beloved; if, then, Christ lives in you and you in Christ, follow him in your life, in words, works and sufferings. Be meek and merciful, pitiful, kind and well-disposed to all who seek your help. Hate none, envy none, despise none, nor vex any with hard words; but forgive all. Jeer not at any man, nor show contempt, whether by word or deed, by sign or attitude, or in any way whatever. Be not stubborn, nor sour, but let your bearing be seemly, and your countenance cheerful. Be ready to hear and learn, no matter of whom whatever you should know. Misjudge nobody, nor judge rashly of that which is hid from you. Enter not into dispute with any, therein showing yourself wiser than he. Be meek as the lamb which cannot be angry even when it is slaughtered; and so let be, and keep silence, whatever men may do.' [4]

For many years, in quiet and unobtrusive protest against the worldliness and formalism of much church life around them, Jan van Ruysbroeck, his relative, Jan Hinckaert, and another learned canon, Franco de Coudenberg, had set up house together and lived a very simple and unpretentious life, having all things in common after the manner of the primitive Christian community of the Jerusalem church. In 1343, when van Ruysbroeck was fifty years old, the three of them left Brussels for ever, having decided to seek a life of greater seclusion. They were given the hermitage of Groenendael in the forest of Soignes outside Brussels, where they began almost at once to build a chapel. It was not long before they were joined by others and they decided to seek the protection and stability of a religious community and placed themselves under the Rule of the Augustinian canons, a Rule which had become noted for its sanity and flexibility. In

[4] *The Seven Steps of the Ladder of Spiritual Love.* Tr. F. Sherwood Taylor, Dacre Press, pp. 25–6.

1349 Ruysbroeck took the vows of an Augustinian canon, the hermitage became the priory of Groenendael, and Ruysbroeck became prior. His priory soon established itself as a place of especial sanctity, particularly on account of the personal holiness of its prior. People came from far and near to consult him. It is known that he exercised a profound influence on Gerard Groot, who founded the association of the Brothers of the Common Life, which, although it did not require vows of its members, reached a lofty degree of spirituality and exerted a wide influence, counting Thomas à Kempis, for example, among its members.

The story is told that two students came from Paris to consult van Ruysbroeck concerning their spiritual state. He is reputed to have told them, 'You are as holy as you wish to be.' What he meant was this : 'The measure of your holiness is proportionate to the goodness of your will. Consider then how good your will is, and the degree of your holiness will be clear to you. For every one is as holy, as he is good of heart.' [5]

It is noteworthy that the great masters of the spiritual life, while exhibiting the power of that life in all its fullness, often bear witness to some particular aspect or aspects of its peculiar richness, or set forth with special intensity the meaning of one of the Mysteries of Christ. Of Saint Benedict it might be said that he exemplified the meaning of Christian obedience; of Saint Bernard that he enkindled devotion to the Humanity of Christ; of Saint Francis that he illuminated the meaning of poverty; of Ramon Lull that he bore witness to the power of apostolic love. Seldom, if ever, has any one expounded the positive, all-embracing quality of chastity embraced for the love of Christ, in more beautiful or more convincing terms than van Ruysbroeck. In the chapter, 'Of Purity,' in the *Adornment of the Spiritual Marriage,* the spiritual principles underlying the practice of chastity are so drawn out that it is shown in its true nature as a warm and attractive virtue, and so that it is readily seen how the blessing promised to those who keep it untarnished is no less than the vision of

[5] *The Seven Steps,* p. 15.

God himself, which is the ultimate goal of the spiritual life. For the depth of its insights and for the simplicity and beauty of the language, van Ruysbroeck's exposition is worth quoting at length :

'Purity of spirit is this : that a man should not cleave to any creature with desirous affection, but to God alone; for we should use all creatures, but enjoy only God. Purity of spirit makes a man cleave to God, above all understanding, and above all feelings, and above all the gifts which God may pour into his soul; for all that a creature receives in his understanding and in his feeling, purity will pass by, to rest in God. Go therefore to the Sacrament of the Altar, . . . not for anything else than the glory of God and your own growth in all virtues. This is purity of spirit.

'Purity of heart is this : that a man, in every bodily temptation or natural inclination, of his own free will, and with an ever-renewed confidence and without hesitation, turns to God; with an ever-renewed faithfulness and with a firm will ever to remain with him. For consenting to those sins or satisfactions, which the bodily nature seeks like a beast, is a departure from God.

'Purity of body is : that a man withdraws from, and bewares of, all unchaste deeds, in whatsoever manner they be, which his conscience teaches and declares to be unchaste, and contrary to the commandments, the honour, and the will of God.

'By these three kinds of purity the seventh mortal sin is overcome and cast out; that is, Unchastity . . .

'Now you should know that purity of spirit keeps a man in the likeness of God, untroubled by any creature, and inclined towards God, and united with him.

'Purity of body is likened to the whiteness of lilies and the cleanness of the angels. In withstanding, it is likened to the redness of roses and to the nobleness of martyrs. If it is kept for the love and the glory of God, it is perfect. And so it is likened to the sunflower, for it is one of the highest ornaments of nature.

'Purity of heart works a renewal and increase of the grace of God. By purity of heart all the virtues are prompted, practised and preserved. It guards and keeps the senses from without; it quells and restrains the animal lusts from within; it is an adornment of all inwardness. And it is the door of the heart; barred against all earthly things and all deceit, but opened to all heavenly things and to all truth. And of all such Christ says : BLESSED ARE THE PURE IN HEART : FOR THEY SHALL SEE GOD; and in this vision consist our eternal joy, our reward and our entrance into bliss. Therefore men should be sober and temperate in all things, and beware of all intercourse and occasion whereby purity, whether of soul or body may be defiled.'

During the thirty-eight years of his stay at Groenendael Jan van Ruysbroeck wrote the majority of his books and certainly the greatest of them. He wrote all his works in his native Brabant, eleven of which have come down to us in various manuscript collections. A standard Latin translation was made by the Carthusian monk, Laurentius Surius, in the sixteenth century. Best known to the modern English reader, probably, are the *Adornment of the Spiritual Marriage,* the *Sparkling Stone,* the *Book of Supreme Truth,* and the *Seven Steps of the Ladder of Spiritual Love.* The title of the last-named book describes the cardinal theme of all his important books, namely the growth and development of the soul in its movement and progress towards God and that union with God for which it was created. Sometimes his terminology varies. In the *Adornment of the Spiritual Marriage,* for example, he speaks of three stages in the soul's progress, the Active, the Interior and the Superessential or Supernatural life; whereas in the *Sparkling Stone,* he speaks of three states, that of the Servant, the Friend and the Son.

As has already been indicated, one of the most important characteristics of van Ruysbroeck's teaching is that the only stable and enduring foundation for the contemplative, or mystical, life, is the development of the Christian character, or the growth in all virtues. The citations already made from the *Adornment* and from the *Seven Steps* have indicated Ruybroeck's emphasis on the importance of moral training. Indeed, Book One of the *Adorn-*

ment of the Spiritual Marriage and similar sections of his other works may be said to correspond to the Purgative way delineated by Dionysius the Areopagite and other writers on the spiritual life. In all van Ruysbroeck's expositions of this phase of spiritual discipline and training he lays great stress on the importance of having a right intention in addition to keeping himself free from mortal sin and obedient to the commands of God and the Church :

'The third thing which behoves every good man is that in all his deeds he should have in mind, above all else, the glory of God. And if it happens that by reason of his business or the multiplicity of his works, he has not always God before his eyes, yet at least there should be established in him the intention and the desire to live according to the dearest will of God.' [6]

In Ruysbroeck, as in all great masters of the spiritual life, conformity with the will of God is the first step 'on the ladder of love and the holy life.'

The Second Book of the *Adornment of the Spiritual Marriage* corresponds to the description of the Illuminative Way in other writers and portrays the action of God in the soul, or, to use the language of the *Sparkling Stone,* delineates the state of the soul when it makes the transition from servant to a friend of God. Using the imagery of light and fire, the Second Book of the *Adornment* delineates the first form of contemplation, that is, adherence to God by means of the purified reason and will, which results in perfect charity, that is to say, in an outgoing love towards God and the saints, towards all sinners, towards the souls in purgatory, towards a man's own self and towards all men.

The whole of the Second Book of the *Adornment* treats of the ways in which the Spirit of God comes into, and takes possession of, the inner spirit of man. It is clear that the will of man is still active but the separate powers of our nature are being transformed by the action of the Holy Spirit into an essential unity.

[6] *Sparkling Stone,* Ch. i.

This process van Ruysbroeck calls the 'third coming of Christ,' and describes it thus :

'Through this loving inclination of God, and his inward working in the unity of our spirit, and further through our glowing love and the pressing of all our powers together into the very unity in which God dwells, there arises the third coming of Christ in inward working. And this is an inward touch or stirring of Christ in his Divine brightness, in the inmost part of our spirit. . . . For here there is a union of the higher powers within the unity of the spirit, above the multiplicity of all the virtues, and here no one works save God alone, in untrammelled goodness; which is the cause of all our virtues and of all blessedness.' [7]

During this part of the soul's progress one of the dominant characteristics of its spiritual striving is its hunger for God. Dom Vandenbroucke sees this to be so important a part of the *Adornment* that he calls the whole of the second stage of the soul's spiritual advancement, corresponding to the Second Book of the *Adornment,* 'the desire for God.' [8] In a chapter which is reminiscent of the lines in the 'Jesu dulcis memoria' :

> Qui te gustant, esuriunt;
> Qui bibunt, adhuc sitiunt;
>
>> (Celestial sweetness unalloyed;
>> Who eat thee hunger still;
>> Who drink of thee still feel a void,
>> Which nought but thou can fill)

van Ruysbroeck writes movingly and eloquently of the soul's craving for God :

'Here there begins an eternal hunger, which shall never more be satisfied; it is an inward craving and hankering of the loving power and the created spirit after an uncreated Good. And since the spirit longs for fruition, and is invited and urged thereto by God, it must always desire its fulfilment. Behold, here there

[7] *Adornment,* pp. 118–19.
[8] op. cit., p. 482.

begins an eternal craving and continual yearning in eternal in-satiableness. . . . Though God gave to (such) a man all the gifts which are possessed by all the saints, and everything that he is able to give, but withheld himself, the gaping desire of the spirit would remain hungry and unsatisfied. The inward stirring and touching of God makes us hungry and yearning; for the Spirit of God hunts our spirit; and the more it touches it, the greater our hunger and our craving. And this is the life of love in its highest working, above reason and above understanding; for reason can here neither give nor take away from love, for our love is touched by the Divine love. And as I understand it, here there can never more be separation from God. God's touch within us, forasmuch as we feel it, and our own loving craving, these are both created and creaturely, and therefore they may grow and increase as long as we live.' [9]

During this stage of progression in the spiritual life when, to use the terminology of the *Adornment,* the soul is living the Interior life, or, to use the terminology of the *Sparkling Stone,* the soul becomes the secret friend of God, and becomes capable of the next stage of contemplation and enters upon that degree of simple communion with God which Ruysbroeck calls 'the most inward of all exercises.' Of the difference between the 'faithful servants' and the 'secret friends' of God van Ruysbroeck has written thus in the seventh chapter of the *Sparkling Stone:*

'Through grace and the help of God, the faithful servants have chosen to keep the commandments of God, that is, to be obedient to God and Holy Church in all virtues and goodly behaviour; and this is called the outward or active life. But the inward friends of God choose to follow, besides the commandments, the quickening counsels of God; and this is a loving and inward cleaving to God for the sake of his eternal glory, with a willing abandonment of all that one may possess outside God with lust and love. All such friends God calls and invites inwards, and he teaches them the distinctions of inward exercises and many a

[9] *Adornment,* Ch. 53, pp. 121–2.

hidden way of ghostly life. But he sends his servants outwards, that they may be faithful to him and to his House in every service and in every kind of outward good works.

'Behold, thus God gives his grace and his help to each man according to his fitness; that is, according to the way in which he is in tune with God, whether in outward good works or in the inward practice of love. But none can do and feel the inward exercises unless he be wholly turned inward to God.' He then goes on to utter a warning similar to those in the *Adornment* in which he sees the passive doctrines of the Quietists as a caricature of the true peace and surrender of the Interior life. The passage quoted above continues :

'But there are found some foolish men who would be so inward that they would neither act nor serve, even in those things of which their neighbour has need. Behold, these are neither secret friend nor faithful servants of God; but they are altogether false and deceived. For no man can follow the counsels of God who will not keep his commandments. And therefore all secret friends of God are also at the same time faithful servants, wherever this is needful; but all the faithful servants are not secret friends, for the exercise which belongs thereto is unknown to them.'

The Third Book of the *Adornment of the Spiritual Marriage,* the last chapters of the *Sparkling Stone* and of the *Book of Supreme Truth* as well as the seventh step of the *Ladder of Spiritual Love* all describe, although with different terminology the highest stages of contemplation, when the soul enters upon the 'superessential' or 'deified' life and becomes not only the servant and friend but also the son of God. The life of Union is also described by van Ruysbroeck as the 'life of the God-seeing man,' in which the soul enters upon a new and permanent state of deepened intimacy with God. In all Ruysbroeck's writings the relation of the soul to God is based upon an analogy between the life of the Blessed Trinity. The life of union is neither passive nor static, but active, creative and full of movement. Of the many passages that might be chosen to illustrate this aspect of Ruysbroeck's thought one must suffice; notably the chapter in which he speaks of 'a Divine Meeting which Takes Place in the Hiddenness of our Spirit':

'Now this rapturous meeting is incessantly and actively renewed in us, according to the way of God; for the Father gives himself in the Son, and the Son gives himself in the Father, in an eternal content and a loving embrace; and this renews itself every moment in the bonds of love. For like as the Father incessantly beholds all things in the birth of his Son, so all things are loved anew by the Father and the Son in the outpouring of the Holy Ghost. And this is the active meeting of the Father and of the Son, in which we are lovingly embraced by the Holy Ghost in eternal love.'

The above passage reminds us that any true apprehension of the Divine Unity may not cancel or blur the distinctions of Persons and Relations in the Holy Trinity, for those distinctions are absolute and eternal. In a similar way van Ruysbroeck is emphatic that the unified or 'deified' life of the soul with God, which is its ultimate and final goal, can never involve or imply the annihilation of the self. When he speaks of the soul feeling itself to be one with the truth, the richness and the unity of God, he goes on to say, 'Yet even here there is an essential distinction between the being of the soul and the being of God; and this is the highest and finest distinction we are able to feel.' [10]

The perfect life of union, as far as man is able to attain it in this life, is sometimes called the universal life by van Ruysbroeck, because for him the highest stages of contemplation comprise both prayer and action. Not only action but suffering also. In the fourth step of the *Ladder of Spiritual Love,* he had described patient suffering as 'the wedding-garment which Christ put on when he took his Church as bride at the altar of the Holy Cross, and with the same garment he has clothed all the family—those who have followed him since the beginning.' [11] The significance

[10] *Adornment,* Bk. 3, Ch. 4, p. 177.   [11] p. 26.

of action and suffering in the life of the God-seeing man is beautifully expressed in the fourteenth chapter of the *Sparkling Stone:*

'The man who is sent down by God from these heights into the world is full of truth and rich in all virtues. And he seeks not his own but the glory of him that sent him. And hence he is just and truthful in all things, and he possesses a rich and generous ground, which is set in the richness of God; and therefore he must always spend himself on those who have need of him; for the living fount of the Holy Ghost, which is his wealth, can never be spent. And he is a living and willing instrument of God, with which God works and whatsoever he wills and howsoever he wills; and these works he reckons not as his own, but gives all the glory to God. And so he remains ready and willing to do in the virtues all that God commands, and strong and courageous in suffering and enduring all that God allows to befall him. And by this he possesses a universal life, for he is ready alike for contemplation and for action, and is perfect in both of them.' [12]

However much progress in the spiritual life may be a question of mounting and not merely of going on, it is important to remember that the *Seven Steps of the Ladder of Spiritual Love* cannot be regarded, as a recent editor points out, as 'so many graded exercises for the obtaining of the gift of contemplation.' [13] Van Ruysbroeck, as we have seen, never minimized the importance of the human will and the part that it has to play in cooperation with the operation of divine grace within the soul. Nevertheless he never fails to make clear that all spiritual graces including the highest activities of prayer and contemplation are gifts of God. Moreover, van Ruysbroeck has especially pointed out that in the higher stages of prayer, as the soul's relationship with God becomes deeper the more methodless it also becomes, for it finds itself treading a way that is wayless. Indeed, he

[12] pp. 220–1.
[13] Joseph Bolland, S.J., p. 2.

describes contemplation as being 'the simple staring with open heart into the Divine Brightness . . . the wayless passing, and the glorious wandering in the Supernatural Love, wherein neither end, nor beginning, nor way, nor manner can ever be found.' [14]

Of those who read van Ruysbroeck's writings many will find difficulty in understanding and interpreting such passages as the seventh step of the *Ladder of Spiritual Love;* and many will not reach the high levels of contemplative prayer which he described out of his own experience; but all who persevere in the way of perfection appropriate to themselves and to which God has called them, will enter into the inheritance of which van Ruysbroeck speaks almost at the end of the *Book of Supreme Truth:*

'If we will go with God upon the highway of love, we shall rest with him eternally and without end; and thus we shall eternally go forth towards God and enter into him and rest in him.' [15]

[14] *Sparkling Stone,* Ch. 8, p. 198.
[15] p. 48.

CHAPTER 6

SAINT TERESA OF AVILA
1515–1582

WITHIN the confines of a single chapter none but the merest outline can be given of one who was at once saint, mystic, practical business woman, writer, shrewd psychologist (if the term were not an anachronism in the sixteenth century), and Mother foundress, whose dominant personality influenced all with whom she came in contact and stamped itself upon her writings and foundations. For such was Saint Teresa of Avila, Mother of Carmel.

In the Golden Age of Spanish Mysticism, which was as brilliant and translucent as it was shortlived, Saint Teresa is generally claimed to be the most outstanding of the Spanish mystics. Paradoxically it may be, but just as certainly, her writings, after four hundred years, continue to make a wide and popular appeal to many who, although they will never live under the discipline of the Carmelite Rule because such is not their vocation, have discovered, nevertheless, or desire to discover, as did Elijah of old on the veritable Mount Carmel, that God is to be found not in the wind, the earthquake or the fire, but in the 'still, small voice' of the life of prayer and interior silence. The secret of her wide appeal is disclosed by one of the greatest of her modern interpreters, the late Professor E. Allison Peers, when he wrote : 'She is a mystic—and more than a mystic. Her works, it is true, are well known in the cloister and have served as nourishment to many who are far advanced on the Way of Perfection, and who, without her aid, would still be beginners in the life of prayer. Yet they have also entered the homes of millions living in the world and have brought consolation, assurance, hope, and strength to souls who, in the technical sense, know nothing of the life of contemplation. Devoting herself, as she

97

did with the most wonderful persistence and tenacity, to the sublimest task given to man—the attempt to guide others to perfection—she succeeded so well in that task that she is respected everywhere as an exceedingly gifted teacher, who has revealed, more, perhaps, than any who came before her, the nature and the extent of those gifts which the Lord has laid up in this life for those who love him.' [1]

This book purports to be in no sense a treatise on Mystical Theology, and in this book and its companion volumes, *A City Not Forsaken* and *If Any Man Build,* the use of technical theological terms and arguments has been avoided as far as possible, yet something must here be said about the word 'mystic' and its cognate terms, 'mystical' and 'mysticism,' terms which have not only been used in widely differing contexts in the long history of Christian literature, but which have also given rise to some sharp controversies amongst theologians and writers on the spiritual life in different historical circumstances and in different Christian traditions. In the first place, the use of the word 'mystical' in the Pauline Epistles refers to the, if one may coin the word, 'churchly' Body of Christ. In the writings of the Early Fathers of the Church the term 'mystical Body' is used to designate not the Church but the sacramental Body of Christ. It is no part of our present purpose to discuss the diverse definitions of the word 'mysticism' as it applies to the life of prayer and contemplation, but for the sake of clarity a few observations may be made. Within the scope of this book and its companion volumes it has been sufficient to define the spiritual life, as the Christian understands it, in broad terms as a life of communion with God through Christ in the power of the Holy Spirit. Within such a definition are to be found the criteria both of the validity and the relevance of Christian mysticism. Amongst those English and European masters of the spiritual life chosen for study in this present series, it will be apparent that some may be described as mystics and some not. The extent to which visions, ecstasies and

[1] E. A. Peers, *Works,* I, p. xxxvii.

other common phenomena of mystical experience are essential components of it has often been in debate, but it is worth noting both that such experiences were vouchsafed to some of the New Testament writers, notably Saint John and Saint Paul,[2] and that many mystics themselves have repudiated the idea that such experiences were of the essence of the mystical life. Although the charge of pantheism has not infrequently been laid against Christian mystics, the idea of the union of the soul with God, which may be said to be the principal tenet of mysticism, involves man neither in a particular form of pantheism nor in the destruction of man's creaturely status, a fact which has often been illustrated in these three volumes from the writings of the mystics themselves.

Because the mystical element in religion presupposes the possibility of the human soul to enter into direct and personal communion, if not union with God, the charge of individualism is often laid against it. But, as I have pointed out elsewhere,[3] 'the experience of the contemplative has a relevance to the life of the Church as a whole. For Christian mysticism does not concern the individual soul and God alone. For the individual Christian, by reason of his status as a baptized member of the Body of Christ, the Church, be he mystic or not, "does not come to God like the pagan, as the alone to the Alone." [4] The experience of the contemplative has a significance extending far beyond the confines of his own religious consciousness, and his very existence carries a constant reminder of the fact that the very meaning and purpose of the Christian life is union with God in Christ. "What is essential to the Christian life is union with God by faith, hope and charity; it is because the mystic has been given an extraordinary insight into the nature of that union that his utterances are relevant not only to other mystics but to the Church as a whole." ' [5] Nevertheless, there remains a certain reluctance to

[2] See *If Any Man Build.*
[3] *A Living Sacrifice,* S.C.M. Press, p. 121.
[4] G. Dix, *The Shape of the Liturgy,* 1949 ed., p. x.
[5] E. L. Mascall, *Via Media,* 1956, p. 136.

employ the term 'mystic' for the reason advanced by Professor Peers : 'I often wish there were some word in the English language which we could substitute for the word "mysticism," for as long as it continues to be used, the non-instructed reader will associate it with mistiness; and there never was less mistiness anywhere than in those practical, determined and clear-cut persons, the mystics, among whom none has these qualities in more generous measure than Saint Teresa.' [6]

Teresa de Cepeda y Ahumada was born in Avila, a fortress-like town on the bare Castilian plateau, in 1515, and many of her biographers have drawn an apt comparison between the strength and austerity of its surroundings and its architecture and the flint-like qualities, masculine courage and rugged perseverance of the greatest of its daughters. Teresa was born into a large family who lived, however, in circumstances not of austerity, but of comfort and culture. The stories told of her childhood show her to have displayed those qualities of initiative, imagination, courage and religious devotion which were to characterize her long and outstanding life. After the death of her beautiful mother in 1528, she entered an Augustinian convent as a boarder, where she stayed for about eighteen months. If the autobiographical notice in her *Spiritual Relations* can be depended upon —'It is forty years since this nun took the habit'—she entered the Convent of the Incarnation, Avila, a house of the Carmelite Order, in 1536, where she was professed the following year.

Less than two years after her profession she was assailed by a severe illness which caused her to spend a good part of the time during the next few years away from her convent, either at the home of her half-sister, or undergoing treatment. Even after her return to the convent in 1540, she was an invalid for more than a year, and she suffered intermittent attacks of paralysis till about 1554. Many who have had to face grievous and prolonged physical suffering have found consolation and inspiration from Saint Teresa's attitude to her sufferings :

[6] *Saint Teresa of Jesus and Other Essays and Addresses,* 1953, p. 17.

'For when I found that, while still so young, I was so seriously paralysed, and that earthly doctors had been unable to cure me, I resolved to seek a cure from heavenly doctors, for, though I bore my sickness with great joy, I none the less desired to be well again. I often reflected that, if I were to grow well and then incur damnation, it would be better for me to remain as I was; but still I believed that I should serve God much better if I recovered my health. That is the mistake we make; we do not leave ourselves entirely in the Lord's hands; yet he knows best what is good for us.' [7]

Between the death of her father, which was a great grief to her, and what is sometimes called her 'second conversion' in 1557, practically nothing is known of her life. From 1555 she had begun to experience a renewed sense of the presence of God and, as she herself expressed it, to be 'addressed by interior voices and to see certain visions and experience revelations.' After what she described as 'nearly twenty years on that stormy sea,' she had reached a degree of spiritual certainty and maturity, which were to be but the foundation of further advances, for it was not long after that she experienced her first rapture and also began to discuss the foundation in Avila of a convent of discalced nuns, who would inaugurate a stricter and reformed obedience to the Carmelite Rule. Space does not permit the present author to describe the many difficulties which surrounded such a venture, but eventually she achieved her purpose and her first foundation, that of the convent of Saint Joseph at Avila, came into being on August 24th, 1562. In the following year, she was granted permission to transfer her house of residence from the Incarnation to Saint Joseph's. The years that she spent at Saint Joseph's from 1562–7 she was later to call 'the most restful years of my life.'

It is not possible in this short biographical sketch to describe the train of events which led her to make seventeen foundations of the Reform. Of the underlying spiritual motives she has written movingly in the *Way of Perfection,* showing herself to be not

[7] *Works,* I, p. 34.

only deeply concerned for the principles of the Religious Life but also of the Counter-Reformation :

'And, seeing that I was a woman, and a sinner, and incapable of doing all I should like in the Lord's service, and as my whole yearning was, and still is, that, as he has so many enemies and so few friends, these last should be trusty ones, I determined to do the little that was in me—namely, to follow the evangelical counsels as perfectly as I could, and to see that these few nuns who are here should do the same, confiding in the great goodness of God, who never fails to help those who resolve to forsake everything for his sake. As they are all that I ever imagined them as being in my desires, I hoped that their virtues would more than counteract my defects, and I should thus be able to give the Lord some pleasure, and all of us, by busying ourselves in prayer for those who are defenders of the Church, and for the preachers and learned men who defend her, should do everything we could to aid this Lord of mine who is so much oppressed by those to whom he has shown so much good that it seems as though these traitors would send him to the Cross again and that he would have nowhere to lay his head.' [8]

The seventeen convents of the Reform involved the Mother Foundress in many long and arduous journeys, and in many difficult visitations which called forth all her magnificent reserves of gay courage, dogged perseverance and spiritual stability. Julian de Avila, who accompanied her wherever she went, writes thus of the trials they experienced on a difficult journey from Beas to Seville :

'These and many other trials which presented themselves, we bore with the greatest joy, for the holy Mother encouraged us every one with her profitable and delightful conversation. Sometimes she would speak of the weightiest subjects; at other times she would say things for our entertainment; sometimes again she would make up verses, and very good ones, for she was most skilful at this, although she did it only when she found her

[8] *Works,* II, p. 4.

material ready to hand. Given though she was, therefore, to prayer, it did not hinder our spiritual intercourse with her from being friendly and beneficial both to the soul and to the body.' [8a]

Despite the saintliness of her life and the attractiveness of her personality the story of her foundations, which continued until a few months before her death with the foundation of the convent at Burgos in April 1582, is a story of conflict and tension, for she incurred hostility and persecution both from within and from without the Carmelite Order. Detailed mention cannot here be made of the troubled course of events which led up to the violent scenes at the election of a Prioress at the Incarnation in 1577, when nuns voting for Saint Teresa were excommunicated; or to the arrest and imprisonment at the instigation of the friars of the Observance of Saint John of the Cross, who was at that time confessor at the convent of the Incarnation; or to the separation of the Calced and Discalced Carmelites, that is to say, of the Observance and the Reform, which became operative in 1581. Typical of the saint's attitude to the many trials and persecutions which she had to undergo are the following lines which she wrote on the fly-leaf of her breviary, which is in possession of the Discalced Carmelite nuns of Medina del Campo:

'Learn of me, for I am meek and humble.

'Saint Chrysostom: Perfect martyrdom is not accomplished by the shedding of blood alone. Martyrdom also consists in true abstinence from sin and in the practice and observance of the commandments of God. True patience in adversities also makes a person a martyr.

'It is union of our will with the will of God that gives our will its value, for it will then desire nothing save that which is the will of his Majesty.

'To have this charity in perfection is glory.' [9]

Had Saint Teresa died in 1567, says her biographer, 'she would have been forgotten save in the annals of Carmel; but she lived fifteen years longer and her name is known in every corner of

[8a] *Vida de Santa Teresa*, cited in Peers: *Works*, III, p. xii.
[9] *Works*, p. 269.

the Christian world.' [10] It is through her writings that she is now known and loved, for the layman and Religious, the simple and the learned, the beginner in the life of prayer and those who can enter with the saint herself into the sixth and seventh mansions of the soul, all alike turn to her for guidance, assurance and direction. For 'to Saint Teresa it was given to speak to the world, in her diaphanous, colloquial language and her simple, unaffected style, of the work of the Holy Spirit in the enamoured soul, of the interior strife and the continual purgation through which a soul must pass in its ascent of Mount Carmel and of the wonders that await it on the mountain's summit.

'So she leads the soul from the rudimentary stages of the Purgative Way to the very heights of Union, bringing it into the innermost mansion of the Interior Castle, where, undisturbed by the foes that rage without, it can have fruition of union with the Lord of that Castle and experience a foretaste of the Beatific Vision of the life to come. But, despite the loftiness and sublimity of these themes, she is able to develop them without ever losing the most attractive of her qualities as a writer—simplicity. Continually she finds ready to hand apt and graphic comparisons, intelligible even to the unlearned. No mystical writer before her day, from the pseudo-Dionysius to Ruysbroeck, nor any who has written since, had described such high matters in a way so apt, so natural and to such a large extent within the reach of all. The publication of her treatises inaugurated for the mystics an epoch of what may almost be called popularity. Those who love the pages of the Gospels, and whose aim in life is to attain the Gospel ideal of perfection, have found in her works other pages in which, without any great effort of the intellect, they may learn much concerning the way. Her practical insistence upon the virtuous life, her faithfulness to the Evangelical counsels and the soundness of her doctrine even in the most obscure and recondite details—all these will commend her to them. Many, indeed, are the fervent lovers of our Lord who have gone

[10] E. A. Peers, *Mother of Carmel,* S.C.M. Press, p. 38.

to the school of love kept by the Foundress of Avila.' [11]

Paradoxically enough, her works were not written originally for publication, but either in obedience to her confessors and spiritual directors, or for the edification, instruction and consolation of her spiritual daughters. Her *Life* which is one of the most readable and at the same time one of the most illuminating of the saint's works, written between 1562 and 1565, was written at the command of her confessors. It is a spiritual autobiography, as it were, rather than a record of external events, even though these latter are not lacking especially in the first part of the work. The first ten chapters deal with the saint's exterior and interior life from the time of her birth till that of her 'second conversion.' After a long digression on mental prayer, chapter XXIII begins, 'I will now return to the place where I left off the description of my life.' It is not long, however, before she digresses again, on to the subject of locutions, until she returns to the subject of her life in chapter XXVIII. The last part of the *Life,* which treats mainly of the foundation at Saint Joseph's, places the emphasis mainly on the interior life.

The digression which begins with chapter XI of the *Life* contains some of the best known and best loved of the saint's expositions. This chapter describes the first stages of the life of prayer under the similitude of the watered garden :

'The beginner must think of himself as of one setting out to make a garden in which the Lord is to take his delight, yet in soil most unfruitful and full of weeds. His Majesty uproots the weeds and will set good plants in their stead. Let us suppose that this is already done—that a soul has resolved to practise prayer and has already begun to do so. We have now, by God's help, like good gardeners to make these plants grow, and to water them carefully so that they may not perish, but may produce flowers which shall send forth great fragrance to give refreshment to this Lord of ours, so that he may often come into the garden to take his pleasure and have his delight among these virtues.

[11] *Works,* I, pp. xxxvii–viii.

'Let us now consider how this garden can be watered, so that we may know what we have to do, what labour it will cost us, if the gain will outweigh the labour and for how long this labour must be borne. It seems to me that the garden can be watered in four ways; by taking the water from a well, which costs us great labour; or by a water-wheel and buckets, when the water is drawn by a windlass (I have sometimes drawn it in this way; it is less laborious than the other and gives more water); or by a stream or a brook, which waters the ground much better, for it saturates it much more thoroughly and there is less need to water it often, so that the gardener's labour is much less; or by heavy rain, when the Lord waters it with no labour of ours, a way incomparably better than any of those which have been described.' [12]

She then goes on to show how these four different ways of watering the garden correspond to four steps of prayer. Knowing full well that for beginners prayer is 'a very laborious proceeding,' the Mother Foundress shows great understanding of the difficulties arising from distractions and aridity, from dislike and distaste. The beginner is encouraged to persevere in the remembrance that 'he is pleasing and serving the Lord of the garden.' In dealing with the many and varied temptations which continue to beset the beginner the saint's counsels are full of practical common sense as well as of profound spiritual insight, as for example, 'It is of great importance, when we begin to practise prayer, not to let ourselves be frightened by our own thoughts.' [13]

The second degree of prayer, the water wheel, represents that state of recollection known as the Prayer of Quiet, in which the understanding and the memory, though not the will, are, so to speak, at rest, so that the action of God may work directly upon the soul. We do well to let the saint describe it in her own words :

'This state, in which the soul begins to recollect itself, borders on the supernatural, to which it could in no way attain by its own exertions. True, it sometimes seems to have been wearied

[12] *Works*, I, p. 65.
[13] *Works*, I, p. 76.

by its work at the windlass—its labouring with the understanding and its filling of the buckets; but in this state the water is higher and thus much less labour is required than for the drawing of it from the well. I mean that the water is nearer to it, for grace reveals itself to the soul more clearly. This state is a recollecting of the faculties within the soul, so that its fruition of that contentment may be of greater delight. But the faculties are not lost, nor do they sleep. The will alone is occupied in such a way that, without knowing how, it becomes captive. It allows itself to be imprisoned by God, as one who well knows itself to be the captive of him whom it loves. Oh, my Jesus and Lord, how much thy love now means to us! It binds our love so straitly that at that moment it leaves us no freedom to love anything but thee.' 14

In the remainder of this section Saint Teresa gives various counsels concerning the Prayer of Quiet, and observes that 'there are many souls who attain to this prayer and few who pass beyond it.'

Of the third degree of prayer in which the garden is watered by a stream or a spring Saint Teresa wrote: 'This irrigates the garden with much less trouble, although a certain amount is caused by the directing of it. But the Lord is now pleased to help the gardener, so that he may almost be said to be the gardener himself, for it is he who does everything.' 15 Of the part played by the soul she says, 'The will has only to consent to the favours which it is enjoying and to submit to all that true Wisdom may be pleased to accomplish in it. . . . In this state I think it is well for the soul to abandon itself wholly into the arms of God.' 16

The fourth degree of prayer, and the highest that Saint Teresa knew when she wrote the *Life*, is still described under the analogy of the watered garden, this time under the figure of rain, a very compelling metaphor in the dry climate of Castile. In describing

14 *Works*, I, pp. 83-4.
15 *Works*, I, p. 96.
16 *Works*, I, pp. 100 and 101.

the nature and effects of this degree of prayer, which is the union of all the faculties with God, the saint emphasizes both the consolations that the soul receives and the need for perseverance, though being mindful of the fact that those who do attain this 'lofty state' do so 'not through our merits but by the Lord's goodness.' She confesses her inability to describe the things of which she writes in technical, theological language, with the result that her expositions abound in a wealth of vivid and simple metaphors, which are so characteristic of her style. Speaking, for example of the soul's growth in humility at this stage she says : 'It also sees clearly how extremely unworthy it is—for in a room bathed in sunlight not a cobweb can remain hidden.' [17]

It is the practice of modern editors of the saint's works to follow the procedure adopted by her first editor, and to print the 'Spiritual Relations' as an appendix to her spiritual autobiography, for the 'Spiritual Relations' are a group of narratives varying in length from a few lines to a few pages each, and which record a diversity of her personal experiences. It is from this source that her biographers have drawn a number of anecdotes and a number of notices which have been important in the controversies surrounding the dating of major events in the saint's life. For example, the fourth 'Relation' written from Seville in 1576, begins with the words 'It is forty years since this nun took the habit.' [18] From the thirty-fifth 'Relation' comes the well-known story of how Saint John of the Cross, when he was confessor to the Incarnation convent at Avila, one day divided the sacred Host between Saint Teresa and another sister when he was communicating them. The saint's comment on the incident was : 'I thought he was doing this to mortify me, for I had told him that I was very pleased when the Hosts were large ones, though I knew I should be receiving the Lord, whole and entire, if I took only the smallest particle.' [19]

17 *Works,* I, p. 112.
18 *Works,* I, p. 319.
19 *Works,* I, p. 351.

Reference has already been made to the *Way of Perfection* in which Saint Teresa described the motives which inspired her first foundation. The book itself was begun in 1565, and it was written to comply with the earnest request of the nuns of the first convent of the Reform. After three introductory chapters, the next part of the book, chapters IV–XV, treats of the principles underlying adherence to the Rule and Constitutions of the Order, the most important being mutual love, detachment from created things and true humility. The next chapters (XVI–XXVI), expound what is meant by the contemplative life and may be read with great profit by beginners on what the saint calls 'the road of Prayer' as well as by those who have made considerable advancement. This section contains Saint Teresa's famous, and somewhat startling comparison between a game of chess and the life of prayer and contemplation. Before coming to the similitude of the game itself, in which the soul gives check and mate to the King of love, Jesus, she writes about the placing of the pieces, for 'you may be sure that any one who cannot set out the pieces in a game of chess will never be able to play well, and, if he does not know how to give check, he will not be able to bring about a checkmate.' [20] In all Saint Teresa's writings there is an extraordinary mixture of the sublime and the practical, as in the following passage, for example, where she counsels : 'Remember that there must be someone to cook the meals and count yourselves happy in being able to serve like Martha. Reflect that true humility consists to a great extent in being ready for what the Lord desires to do with you and happy that he should do it, and in always considering yourselves unworthy to be called his servants. If contemplation and vocal and mental prayer and tending the sick and serving in the house and working at even the lowliest tasks are of service to the Guest who comes to stay with us and to eat and take his recreation with us, what should it matter to us if we do one of these things rather than another.' [21]

[20] *Works*, II, p. 63.
[21] *Works*, II, p. 71.

The first two sections of the *Way of Perfection* lead up to the last section, chapters XXVII–XLII, which comprise a commentary on the Lord's Prayer, touching incidentally on the saint's master-themes of Recollection, Quiet and Union. This section affords countless examples of the saint's free, colloquial and almost familiar way of addressing God in ejaculatory prayer. There was no false humility and no mere conventionality in Saint Teresa's approach to God. 'Avoid being bashful with God,' she says, 'as some people are, in the belief that they are being humble. It would not be humility on your part if the King were to do you a favour and you refused to accept it; but you would be showing humility by taking it, and by being pleased with it, yet realizing how far you are from deserving it. A fine humility it would be if I had the Emperor of Heaven and earth in my house, coming to it to do me a favour and to delight in my company, and I were so humble that I would not answer his questions, nor remain with him, nor accept what he gave me, but left him alone. Or if he were to speak to me and beg me to ask for what I wanted, and I were so humble that I preferred to remain poor and even let him go away, so that He would see that I had not sufficient resolution.

'Have nothing to do with that kind of humility, daughters, but speak with him as a Father, a Brother, a Lord and a Spouse— and, sometimes in one way and sometimes in another, he will teach you what you must do to please him.' [22]

The book of the *Foundations,* which Saint Teresa began in 1573, takes up the story of her career at the point where she left it off at the end of the *Life* and it continues till within a few months of her death. As the title implies, it chiefly describes the foundation of the seventeen new convents of the Reform and the manner of life which the nuns lived within them. A passage such as the following illustrates the joy which accompanied the foundation of a new convent as well as the type of difficulty which also had to be faced, and the practical business acumen of the Mother

[22] *Works,* II, pp. 114–15.

Foundress. It concerns the foundation of the convent of Saint Joseph in the city of Salamanca :

'There was a large congregation, and we had music, and the Most Holy Sacrament was reserved with great solemnity; and, as the house was in a good situation, people got to hear about it and began to esteem it highly. . . . But on the very next day, as if to temper our joy at having the Most Holy Sacrament with us, we were visited by the gentleman who owned the house, and he was so angry that I did not know what to do with him. The devil would not let him listen to reason—for we had fulfilled the whole of our part of the agreement with him . . . but afterwards he changed his mind. So I resolved to let him have his house again, but he did not want that either; what he wanted was immediate payment for it. . . . And in fact, though this happened more than three years ago, the purchase has not been completed, and I do not know if the convent will remain in that house or, if not, where it will go. . . . Our nuns here, by the mercy of God, are very good, and bear everything joyfully. May it please his Majesty to grant them greater progress, for it matters little whether we have a good house or not—indeed, it is a great pleasure for us to find ourselves in a house from which we may at any time be turned out, when we remember that the Lord of the world had no house at all.' [23]

The *Interior Castle,* which Saint Teresa wrote in 1577 with great intensity, is one of the greatest books on mystical theology in existence. It is the most carefully ordered book that the saint ever wrote, although it does not carry the arrangement of the general plan into every chapter, and the saint's naturalness and spontaneity continues to characterize the work. In any case, as Professor Peers has pointed out, it is difficult to say how far ex-periential mysticism can ever lend itself to inflexible scientific rule without endangering its own spirit. Since God is free to establish an ineffable communion with the questing soul, the soul must be free to set down its experiences as they occur to it.' [24]

At the very beginning of the first chapter the saint outlines the

[23] *Works,* III, pp. 96-7.   [24] *Works,* II, p. 189.

idea which was to provide the basis of the whole book, thus : 'I began to think of the soul as if it were a castle made of a single diamond or of very clear crystal, in which there are many rooms, just as in Heaven there are many mansions.' [25] Maintaining the same figure of speech throughout, Saint Teresa traces the soul's progress in the contemplative life from the outer courtyard of the castle to its innermost seventh mansion, 'where the most secret things pass between God and the soul,' [26] and where the soul has been transformed from an imperfect and sinful creature into the Bride of the Spiritual Marriage. Nevertheless, the fact that the castle appears to have 'many mansions, some above, others below, others at each side,' [27] would suggest that different souls advance by different routes and that their experiences at any particular stage of the journey are likely to differ from one another.

The human soul, made in the image and likeness of God, spends a long time undergoing the discipline of the Mansions of Humility. In the Second Mansions the soul takes advantage of every opportunity of spiritual development and learns the practice of Prayer. The soul in the Third Mansions, the Mansions of the Exemplary Life, has many trials to undergo before it reaches the Fourth Mansions, which are identified with the Prayer of Quiet, or the Second Water in the 'life.' Here, however, the saint introduces a fresh thought for she distinguishes a state immediately preceding the Prayer of Quiet, which she calls the prayer of Recollection. In the Fifth Mansions, corresponding to the Third Water, the saint describes the Spiritual Betrothal or Prayer of Union. This she describes under one of the most famous of her simple but extended metaphors, that of the silk-worm; the silk-worm being the contemplative soul, the mulberry leaves being the help it receives from God in the Church until it is full-grown and starts to build the house in which it is to die, its life 'hidden in the greatness of God' :

25 *Works*, II, p. 201.
26 *Works*, II, p. 202.
27 *Works*, II, pp. 202, 207–8.

'When the warm weather comes, and the mulberry-trees begin to show leaf, this seed starts to take life; until it has this sustenance, on which it feeds, it is as dead. The silk-worms feed on the mulberry leaves until they are full-grown, when people put down twigs upon which, with their tiny mouths, they start spinning silk, making themselves very tight little cocoons, in which they bury themselves. Then, finally, the worm, which was large and ugly, comes right out of the cocoon a beautiful white butterfly.' [28]

In the Sixth Mansions the soul experiences both greater favours and greater afflictions until it comes at length to the Seventh Mansions, where it reaches the Spiritual Marriage, where dwells the King. The falling rain becomes merged in the river. The soul reaches a state of perfect peace and joy which can be surpassed only by the Beatific Vision in the Life to come.

Brief and inadequate as this sketch of the saint's life and writings inevitably is, it will have achieved its purpose if it sends the reader to the saint herself, for 'the only way to get to know Saint Teresa is to read her.' [29] We can, however, catch her spirit from some lines found after her death in a breviary which, in the words of a contemporary, 'she was using when our Lord called her to Heaven from Alba,' words which are known in English as 'Saint Teresa's Book-mark' :

> *Let nothing disturb thee;*
> *Let nothing dismay thee;*
> *All things pass;*
> *God never changes.*
> *Patience attains*
> *All that it strives for.*
> *He who has God*
> *Finds he lacks nothing;*
> *God alone suffices.* [30]

[28] *Works*, II, p. 253.
[29] E. A. Peers, *Mother of Carmel*, p. 49.
[30] *Works*, III, p. 288.

H

CHAPTER 7

SAINT JOHN OF THE CROSS
1542–1591

ONE summer's day in 1572 was a happy day for Saint Teresa, when her 'little friar,' as she called him, went to Avila as confessor to the Convent of the Incarnation, where, at this time, Saint Teresa herself was Prioress. Four years earlier she had written from Vallodolid commending her young recruit, who had just taken the vows of the Reform and assumed the name of Saint John of the Cross, to Dom Francisco de Salcedo, a gentleman living in Avila, where he would have to stay on his way to Durelo. Her letter, providing us with a contemporary portrait of the young friar and throwing light on the relationship between the two saints is of the greatest possible interest :

'I beg your Honour to have a talk with this Father and help him in this matter, for though small in stature, I know he is great in God's eyes. We shall certainly miss him sorely here, for he is prudent and well-fitted for our way of life, to which I believe our Lord has called him. There is not a friar but speaks well of him, for his life (in the Order), though short, has been one of great penitence. The Lord seems to be leading him by the hand. We have had some differences about business matters; I myself have been at fault and have sometimes been vexed with him, but we have never seen the least imperfection in him.' [1]

To outline the life of Saint John of the Cross is to trace the steps whereby the Lord led him by the hand along the road of suffering love until, having scaled the heights of contemplation, he glorified God by a death akin to martyrdom. Juan de Yepes was born at Fontiveros, some thirty miles north-west of Avila in 1542. After the death of his father some seven years later, his

[1] Quoted E. A. Peers, *St. Teresa of Jesus,* Faber and Faber, 1953, p. 50.

mother and her two sons removed first to Arévalo, and later to the then busy town of Medina del Campo. His mother, a weaver, expected her son to learn a trade and he tried carpentry, tailoring, sculpture and painting by turns. His ability lay in none of these directions, however, and eventually he was sent to school, to the College of the Children of Doctrine in Medina.

The marked scholastic ability of the young Juan brought him to the notice of Don Antonio Alvarez de Toledo, who adopted him. Juan was about fourteen at the time and for the next five years or so he studied at a school recently founded by the Jesuits and also worked in the hospital where his patron was warden. It was evidently the hope of Don Alvarez that his young protége should take Holy Orders and return as chaplain to the hospital where he himself had retired. In 1563, however, at the age of twenty-one, instead of training for the secular priesthood or becoming a Jesuit, he took the habit of the Order of Carmel and the name of John of Saint Matthias in the monastery at Medina, where he was professed the following year.

A few months after his profession John of Saint Matthias entered the University of Salamanca, where, besides reading Arts he also studied theology after his ordination to the priesthood in 1567. He read widely and deeply, and thoroughly assimilated what he read. When he came to write his own treatises he brought to his task not only the enrichment of his wide reading, but the mind and methods of a scholar, enabling him to write with definitiveness and clarity, and to handle even the most abstruse and controversial subjects with a mastery that led his great twentieth exponent, especially for English readers, the late Professor Peers, to make the following observation : 'We may describe the treatises of Saint John of the Cross as the true Summa Angelica of mystical theology.' [2]

It was very soon after his ordination that the young scholarly friar met for the first time Saint Teresa of Avila, a meeting which not only made a lifelong influence on both of them, but also on

[2] *Works,* I, p. xlvi.

the whole future of the Reformed Carmelite Order, and on the history of the whole Church as far as the Contemplative life is concerned. Exactly how they came to meet is not known, but their meeting may well be seen by the eyes of faith to have been arranged by the workings of divine Providence. Saint Teresa, who was fifty-two at the time, was devoting a good deal of thought as to how she could extend the Reform of the Carmelite Order to men's houses, and John of Saint Matthias, with all the enthusiasm of a young man of twenty-five, was seeking a stricter life of spiritual discipline, and was thinking of transferring to the Carthusian Order. In 1568, however, with two other companions, both Carmelites, John of Saint Matthias took the vows of the Reform at Durelo and changed his name to John of the Cross.

The very names of the first men's house of the Reform, Anthony of Jesus, Joseph of Christ and John of the Cross, bore witness to their resolve to know nothing except Jesus and him crucified. Their life at Durelo was one of extreme poverty and austerity, of simplicity and happiness, and their time was spent in reciting the choir offices, standing in the centre of the loft because only so could they stand upright; in prayer and in silence; and in evangelizing the surrounding villages. In 1570 the Durelo monastery was transferred to Mancera. In the same year St. John of the Cross founded the second monastery of the Reform at Pastrana, in the following year he founded a third at Henares, and in the next year, as has been stated, he went to Avila as confessor to the nuns at the Incarnation Convent.

This period in the life of Saint John of the Cross, from 1572–7, while he remained at Avila, although it began so happily was destined to become for him a period of intense suffering, for it was during this time that the hostility between the Calced and Discalced Carmelites became increasingly open and bitter. To those of us who live in an age when not only Christians of the same denomination but also those of other traditions are trying to draw closer together in supernatural love and mutual understanding, it is hard to visualize the savagery with which the

Calced Carmelites persecuted the Discalced Carmelites; or to imagine the circumstances in which, on the night of December 3rd–4th, 1577, Saint John of the Cross was carried off by the Calced as a prisoner to the Calced Carmelite monastery at Toledo. There he was imprisoned in a cell ten feet by six, which, as Saint Teresa wrote in a letter, was 'hardly large enough to hold him, small as he is.' Of the indignities and sufferings to which he was subjected Professor Peers has given a graphic description in his now classic biography of the saint:

'His cell had no outside window—only a hole high in the wall connecting it with a large room which adjoined it. Except on the rare occasions when he was allowed a small oil lamp, the prisoner had to stand on a bench to get light enough to read his breviary, and even this was possible only when the sun was shining into a gallery at one end of the outer apartment. For the eight and a half months of his incarceration, which included the worst part of the Castilian summer, he had no change of clothing. His food was bread and water, with occasional scraps of salt fish. At first, he was made to eat this meal every evening on the floor of the refectory, after which he would bare his shoulders for the penance known as the "circular discipline." Sadistic as it sounds, this was as common a punishment at that time in religious houses as incarceration. The friars would walk round him in a circle, each striking him with a whip as he passed, and handing it to the next in order. After a time they grew tired of this pastime, and indulged in it only twice or thrice weekly, then once weekly, and finally, from May onwards, at rare and irregular intervals.' [3]

No wonder Saint Teresa herself, whose own share of suffering was of a degree and an intensity far above the average, exclaimed, 'I don't know how God tolerates such things,' when she heard about it afterwards. For Saint Teresa and for Saint John of the Cross intense physical, mental and spiritual suffering only served to bring them nearer to God. With no human help and no material consolation Saint John of the Cross lived out the mean-

[3] *Spirit of Flame,* pp. 43–4.

ing of the name he had taken at his profession. He was thrown back entirely upon God, and by entrusting himself utterly to him, he entered, like many another saint before and after him, into the mystery of the Passion, which became for him in the crucible of experience an 'open secret.' Out of his own experience Saint John of the Cross speaks across the centuries to all who suffer for Christ, and to all who seek to unite their sufferings to the passion of Christ, and who find by so doing the 'Peace of God which passeth all understanding,' or, as the present Archbishop of Canterbury is wont to translate it, 'the peace of God which surpasseth all human contrivance.' Many examples could be given from the saint's own writings which demonstrate the way in which, by the grace of God, he transformed his sufferings into 'a living sacrifice,' offered to the praise and glory of God. The following citations are from *Points of Love:*

'Rejoice habitually in God, who is thy salvation, and know that it is good to suffer for him in any way that is good.'

'Crucified inwardly and outwardly with Christ, a man will live in this life with fullness and satisfaction of soul, possessing his soul in his patience.'

'Let Christ crucified be sufficient for thee, and with him do thou suffer and rest; for which cause do thou annihilate thyself with respect to all things, both without and within.'

'Love trials greatly and repute them of small account if thou wilt attain the favour of the Spouse, who hesitated not to die for thee.'

'The soul that walks in love wearies not neither is wearied.'

'He that seeks not the Cross of Christ seeks not the glory of Christ.'

'If a soul becomes more patient in suffering and readier to endure lack of consolations, this is a sign that it is making greater progress in virtue.'

'The purest suffering bears and carries in its train the purest understanding.' [4]

[4] *Works,* III, pp. 250–5. Nos. 5, 8, 13, 15, 18, 23, 41, 48.

One mitigation that the saint was given in prison was that he was allowed paper and ink, and here he composed some of the finest of his poems, as for example, at least the first seventeen verses of the 'Spiritual Canticle,' the poem with the refrain, 'Although 'tis night,' and the stanzas beginning 'in principio erat verbum.' The latter poem, whose English version begins thus:

> *Far away in the beginning*
> *Dwelt the Word of God on high*
> *And in God his bliss eternal*
> *Had he everlastingly* [5]

is only one of very many examples in the saint's poems and treatises which demonstrate his creativeness as a dogmatic as well as a mystical theologian. It is unfortunate that in the history of Christian doctrine the mystics and their teachings have often been held suspect, and often not without cause. No charge of heresy could be levelled against Saint John of the Cross, because his eminence as a dogmatic theologian made it impossible for him to fall into heresy. Of the interdependence between mystical and dogmatic theology in the writings of Saint John of the Cross Professor Peers has written penetratingly as follows:

'The one is, as it were, the lantern that lights the path of the other, as Saint Teresa had realized when she began to feel the continual necessity of consulting theological teachers. If Saint John of the Cross is able to climb the greatest heights of mysticism and remain upon them without stumbling or dizziness it is because his feet are invariably well shod with the truths of dogmatic theology. The great Mysteries—those of the Trinity, the Creation, the Incarnation and the Redemption—and such dogmas as those concerning grace, the gifts of the spirit, the theological virtues, etc., were to him guide-posts for those who attempted to scale, and to lead others to scale, the symbolic mountain of sanctity.' [6]

[5] *Works,* II, p. 455.
[6] *Works,* I, p. xl.

During the month of August 1578, evidently on account of the good offices of a more kindly gaoler, Saint John of the Cross made his escape and stealthily made his way at dead of night to the Reformed convent of Carmelite nuns, who hid him until a certain canon of the cathedral finally got him away to safety. It may be that the opening stanzas of the 'Ascent of Mount Carmel' 'wherein' as the saint himself explains, 'the soul sings of the happy chance it had of passing through the dark night of faith, in detachment and purgation of itself, to union with the Beloved,' were in fact inspired by the events of that memorable night :

1. *On a dark night, Kindled in love with yearnings—oh, happy chance!—*
   I went forth without being observed, My house being now at rest.

2. *In darkness and secure, by the secret ladder, disguised— Oh, happy chance!—*
   In darkness and in concealment, My house being now at rest.

3. *In the happy night, in secret when none saw me, Nor I beheld aught, Without light or guide, save that which burned in my heart.*

4. *This light guided me More surely than the light of noonday,*
   To the place where he (well I knew who!) was awaiting me—
   A place where none appeared.

5. *Oh, night that guided me, Oh, night more lovely than the dawn,*
   Oh, night that joined Beloved with lover, Lover transformed in the Beloved! [7]

At the beginning of October 1578, Saint John of the Cross

[7] *Works*, I, p. 10.

was sent to Monte Calvario as Vicar, in the absence in Rome of the Prior. On his way to Monte Calvario he stayed for a short while at the Carmelite Convent of Beas, whence he returned weekly during his time at Monte Calvario to hear the confessions of the nuns. In their chapel he recited the stanzas of the 'Spiritual Canticle' and his expositions of them in answer to the nuns' questions will have provided the framework for the commentary which he was to write later. His spiritual daughters at Beas were very dear to him and he afterwards kept in touch with them when he could no longer visit them. Of his eighteen extant letters eight are addressed either to individual members of that community or to the community as a whole.

Monte Calvario is the first of the houses in which Saint John of the Cross lived for an extended period. It is here that he is said to have made his original sketch-map of the Mount of Perfection, and here, too, he began his commentaries entitled the 'Ascent of Mount Carmel' and the 'Spiritual Canticle.' These works he continued while he was residing at the Reformed Carmelite house which he founded in 1579. In 1581 he was appointed prior of the Granada Monastery of Los Mártires, where he resided for most of the time until 1588, and where he wrote the last five stanzas of the 'Spiritual Canticle,' finished the 'Ascent of Mount Carmel,' and, in 1585, composed the 'Living Flame of Love,' in fifteen days, at the request of Dôna Ana de Penalosa.

When Saint John of the Cross left Granada in 1588, the violence of the conflict within the Reform itself was about to burst out. This deplorable conflict was brought about largely through the clash of aggressive personalities, Gracian and Doria in particular. Despite his evident sanctity and pacific intentions Saint John of the Cross was caught up into the mesh of opposing forces. So great were the machinations of his enemies that they finally deprived him of his offices. A few months later, in 1591, he fell ill of a fever. The last three months of his life were months of physical suffering and ill-treatment at the hands of the Prior of the House where he was staying. Just before it was too late, however, the Prior came to ask for the saint's forgiveness. On the afternoon of December 14th, 1591, a few months before his fiftieth birthday, Saint John of the Cross knew that his end was near:

' "I shall sing Matins in Heaven," he said at one o'clock. At five: "I am happy, very happy; I shall be in Heaven to-night." Soon afterwards he was again given the Viaticum and sent his brethren away till he called them, so that for the last time he might taste the joys of communion on earth with God. At eleven, he had them summoned, and, raising himself in bed—"most serene, beautiful and happy"—began to recite the *De Profundis*. The brethren made the responses and continued the commendatory prayers for the dying. Suddenly he stopped them. "Read me some verses from the Song of Songs," he begged. The Prior complied. Then, with a crucifix in his hands, he lay back and waited for the stroke of midnight. As the hour began to strike, "It is time for Matins," he said, and, at the first note of the bell, he died.' [8]

More reference must now be made to the writings of the saint. As in the case of Saint Teresa, Saint John of the Cross did not write for publication—indeed none of his works were published until twenty-seven years after his death—but for the edification of his spiritual children, notably the nuns of Beas. It was for them, for example (as has already been stated) that he drew the plan of the Mount of Perfection, which stands as a preface to the 'Ascent of Mount Carmel.' The plan represents a number of graded heights, the highest of which is planted with trees. Of the three paths which lead from the base two denote roads of imperfection, and broad though they are, they peter out before the higher slopes of the mountain are reached. Only the narrow, winding centre path, the path of perfection, leads to the summit and the enjoyment of the heavenly feast. Saint John of the Cross, according to the account of one of his disciples, used to use the 'Mount of Perfection' for giving all kinds of religious counsel:

[8] *Spirit of Flame,* pp. 86–7.

'By means of this drawing, he used to teach us that, in order to attain to perfection, we must not desire the good things of earth, nor those of heaven; but that we must desire naught save to seek and strive after the glory and honour of God our Lord in all things. . . . ' [9]

The plan of the 'Ascent of Mount Carmel' includes within it, strictly speaking, that of the 'Dark Night' and together they set out to describe, as the sub-title to the 'Dark Night' states, 'the method followed by the soul in its journey upon the spiritual road to the attainment of the perfect union of love with God, to the extent that it is possible in this life.' The first line of the poem already quoted, 'On a dark night,' not only gives the name to the second of these two commentaries but also to that particular doctrine of the Dark Night which has made Saint John of the Cross unique in the field of mystical theology, so that he has been called 'the greatest psychologist in the history of mysticism.' [10] The contemplative soul must pass through the Dark Night, that is to say, through a series of purgations, of detachment from creatures and of self-emptying of all that is not God, before it can attain to that union with God, who 'is light and in him there is no darkness at all.'

The first book of the 'Ascent of Mount Carmel' shows how the first obstacles which the soul encounters in its journey towards God are the hindrances which come to it through the senses. Hence the overcoming of these difficulties is called the Night of Sense, and the first thirteen chapters of the 'Ascent' are all a commentary on the first line of the poem, in which the author explains the nature of this Dark Night, describes its causes and stages, and shows how necessary it is for the soul whose quest is union with God. He then goes on, in the memorable thirteenth chapter, to detail the procedure 'which the soul must observe in order to enter this night of sense.' The counsels which he gives illuminate the meaning of detachment as the saint understood it,

[9] Fray Martin de San José. Quoted Peers, I, xxxv.
[10] *Works*, I, xl.

'Strive always to choose, not that which is easiest, but that
which is most difficult;

Not that which is most delectable, but that which is most
unpleasing;

Not that which gives most pleasure, but that which gives
least;

Not that which is restful, but that which is wearisome;

Not that which gives consolation, but rather that which
makes disconsolate;

Not that which is greatest, but that which is least;

Not that which is loftiest, and most precious, but that which
is lowest and most despised; . . .

Strive not to go about seeking the best of temporal things,
but the worst.

Strive thus to enter into complete detachment and emptiness
and poverty, with respect to that which is in the world,
for Christ's sake.' [11]

Book two of the 'Ascent' expounds the second stanza of the
poem already quoted, where the soul enters upon the Night of
Sense, where faith is its surest guide :

'Faith, say the theologians is a habit of soul, certain and
obscure. And the reason for its being an obscure habit is that it
makes us believe truths revealed by God himself, which transcend all natural light, and exceed all human understanding,
beyond all proportion. Hence it follows that, for the soul, this
excessive light of faith which is given to it is thick darkness, for
it overwhelms that which is great and does away with that which
is little, even as the light of the sun overwhelms all other lights
whatever, so that when it shines and disables our powers of vision
they appear not to be lights at all. So that it blinds it and deprives
it of the sight that has been given to it, inasmuch as its light is
great beyond all proportion and surpasses the powers of vision.

[11] *Works,* I, p. 61, § 6.

Even so, the light of faith, by its excessive greatness, oppresses and disables that of the understanding; for the latter, of its own power, extends only to natural knowledge, although it has a faculty for the supernatural, when our Lord may be pleased to bring it to a supernatural action.' [12]

It is during this stage of the soul's pilgrimage that it passes from discursive meditation to contemplation. With the mastery of one who was not only a theologian and a philosopher but also an expert director of souls, Saint John of the Cross describes the three signs which reveal that the soul is ready for this transition :

'The first sign is his realization that he can no longer meditate or reason with his imagination, neither can pleasure therein as he was wont to do aforetime; he rather finds aridity in that which aforetime was wont to attract his senses and to bring him sweetness. But, for as long as he finds sweetness in meditation, and is able to reason, he should not abandon this, save when his soul is led into the peace and quietness which is described under the third head.

'The second sign is a realization that he has no desire to fix his meditation or his sense upon other particular objects, exterior or interior. I do not mean that the imagination neither comes nor goes (for it is wont to move freely even at great times of recollection), but that the soul has no pleasure in fixing it of set purpose upon other objects.

'The third and surest sign is that the soul takes pleasure in being alone, and waits with loving attentiveness upon God, without making any particular meditation, in inward peace and quietness and rest, and without acts and exercises of the faculties —memory, understanding and will—at least, without discursive acts, that is, without passing from one thing to another; the soul is alone, with an attentiveness and a knowledge, general and loving, as we said, but without any particular understanding, and adverting not to what it is contemplating.' [13]

[12] *Works*, I, p. 70, Ch. III, § 1.
[13] *Works*, I, pp. 115–16, § 2, 3, 4.

In the third book of the 'Ascent' the author goes on to describe the obstacles to union with God which come from the memory and the will. This treatise, however, was never finished, and thus it is not possible to emerge with the saint as guide from the Dark Night into the light of day. According to the psychology of Saint John of the Cross, the 'Ascent' is divided into two parts, the 'Active' and the 'Passive' respectively, terminology which is characteristic of the saint's writing as a whole, and which has found its way into the language of mystical theology ever since. Something more must be said, therefore about the use of such terms. As I have pointed out elsewhere [14] :

'One of the chief discussions of the present day in the domain of mystical theology centres round the distinction between "infused" (sometimes called "passive") and "acquired" (sometimes called active) contemplation (although the terms "infused" and "passive," "acquired" and "active" are not altogether synonymous), and posits the question as to the existence of a contemplation which may be called "acquired." It is a disputed point, for example, whether Saint John of the Cross recognized the distinction between "infused" and "acquired" contemplation. Moreover, it is a well-known fact that the term "infused" contemplation is used differently in different traditions. Thus, for example, "for the modern Thomist school, whose procedure is more speculative, the term is extended even to the first stage of contemplation distinguished by Saint John of the Cross, and called in the Teresian school active and acquired contemplation." ' [15] In his penetrating book, *The Venture of Prayer,* Fr. Northcott, C.R., reminds us how misleading such phrases as 'acquired contemplation' and 'infused contemplation' can be. The most important thing is that 'the prayer of contemplation is God-given . . . no amount of natural concentration can produce that strange mysterious something which the soul knows to be the finger of God.' [16]

[14] *A Living Sacrifice,* S.C.M., pp. 119–20.
[15] Fr. Gabriel, *St. John of the Cross, Doctor of Divine Love and Contemplation,* p. 96.
[16] Fr. Northcott, ibid., p. 186.

The Dark Night of the Soul is (as has been observed already), a continuation of the 'Ascent,' in which the Doctor of Divine Love and Contemplation proposes to deal with the Passive Night of Sense and Spirit and to treat of the whole process whereby the soul is transformed into union with God by faith and love, although again the commentary was left unfinished and ends with an exposition of the third stanza, 'In the happy night.'

Space does not permit us to comment at length on the Dark Night, but one might observe that the line with which most MSS. end—'Oh happy night'—serves to illustrate the key-note not only of this work but of all the saint's writing, namely, the happiness of the contemplative life. Despite the trials and sufferings which frequently increase in intensity as the soul advances in the spiritual life, the Dark Night of the Spirit is, nevertheless, a night of happiness because the soul becomes aware that God is leading it to himself by the labyrinthine ways of love, and finds its security in him :

'From what has been said we shall be able to see how this dark night of loving fire, as it purges in the darkness, so also in the darkness enkindles the soul. We shall likewise be able to see that, even as spirits are purged in the next life with dark material fire, so in this life they are purged and cleansed with the dark spiritual fire of love. . . . For cleanness of heart is nothing less than the love and grace of God. For the clean of heart are called by our Saviour "blessed" ; which is as if he had called them "enkindled with love," since blessedness is given by nothing less than love.' [17]

One of the great paradoxes of the Christian life is that the saints have found the direst sufferings to be to them the source of the sublimest joy, and no one more so than Saint John of the Cross. It was while he was in the Toledo dungeon (as has been noted already), that he wrote many of the stanzas of the 'Spiritual Canticle' in which, under the favourite mystical metaphor of the Spouse and the Bride and using much imagery taken from the 'Song of Songs,' he described the highest planes of mystical ex-

[17] *Works,* I, pp. 436–7, § 1.

perience, so that Professor Peers has called his book the 'gift of God to man.' [18] Both the poem and the commentary are, as it were, a dialogue of love, describing the highest and deepest joys which the soul is capable of experiencing in this life, as for example, his exposition of the first words of Stanza XXXV:

> 'Let us rejoice, Beloved, And let us go to see ourselves in thy beauty,
> To the mountain or the hill where flows the pure water; Let us enter farther into the thicket.' [19]

A spirit of joyous happiness also radiates through the poems of Saint John of the Cross, for the lover who has fallen in love with God, so to speak, delights, no less than any other lover, to sing the praises of his Beloved. Notable among his poems is the one entitled 'Song of the soul that rejoices to know God by faith,' with its refrain, 'Although 'tis night,' so characteristic of the saint's thought. The first four stanzas of this poem are given below:

> 'How well I know the fount that freely flows
> Although 'tis night!

> The eternal fount its source has never show'd,
> But well I know wherein is its abode
> Although 'tis night.

> Yea, in a life so sad and dark as this,
> By faith I know the waterspring of bliss,
> Although 'tis night.

> Its origin I know not—it has none;
> All other origins are here begun,
> Although 'tis night.

[18] *Works*, II, p. 8.
[19] *Works*, II, p. 163.

I know that naught beside can be so fair,
That heav'ns and earth drink deep refreshment there,
Although 'tis night.'[20]

The last of the saint's commentaries, the 'living Flame of Love,'
is remarkable in many ways, and not least for the fact that it was
written in fifteen days. The commentary is on four stanzas only,
the first of which runs :

'Oh, living flame of love That tenderly woundest my soul in
its deepest centre,
Since thou art no longer oppressive, perfect me now if it be
thy will, Break the web of this sweet encounter.' [21]

In the Prologue to the commentary, the author explains the nature
of the union between the soul and God under the familiar image
of the log and the fire : 'When a log of wood has been set upon
the fire, it is transformed into fire and united with it; yet, as the
fire grows hotter and the wood remains upon it for a longer time,
it glows much more and becomes more completely enkindled,
until it gives out sparks of flame and fire. And it is of this degree
of enkindled love that the soul must be understood as speaking
when it is at last transformed and perfected interiorly in the fire
of love; not only is it united with this fire but it has now become
one living flame within it.' [22]

Although all may not be able to scale with Saint Teresa's 'little
friar' the top-most peaks of the Mount of Perfection, it remains,
nevertheless, the 'peculiar glory of Saint John of the Cross to have
brought the realms of spiritual adventure, which might have been
thought impossible of encompassment, within the focus of vision
of the ordinary Christian. How much of them he can distinguish,
and in what detail, must depend jointly upon his determination
and his spirituality.' [23]

[20] *Works*, II, p. 454.
[21] *Works*, III, p. 18.

[22] *Works*, III, pp. 16–17.
[23] *Spirit of Flame*, p. 76.

I

CHAPTER 8

SAINT FRANCIS DE SALES
1567–1622

IN this series of studies of great masters of the spiritual life in
Europe, across the countries and down the centuries, an attempt
has been made to demonstrate that the history of Christian
spirituality bears out the truth of the Pauline saying: 'There are
diversities of gifts, but the same spirit.' Of this diversity Saint
Francis de Sales has written simply and effectively at the beginning of his preface to the *Introduction to the Devout Life*.

'The florist Glycera knew so well how to vary the arrangement
and the assortment of flowers that with the same flowers she
made a great variety of bouquets, with the result that the painter
Pausias stopped short, wishing to emulate this diversity of work;
for he did not know how to change his painting in so many ways
as Glycera changed her bouquets: thus the Holy Spirit disposes
and arranges with so much variety the devout instructions which
he gives through the tongues and the pens of his servants, and
while the doctrine remains always the same, their discourses which
they elaborate from it are nevertheless very different, according
to the different ways in which they are composed. I certainly am
not able, nor do I wish, nor ought I to write in this "Introduction" simply what has already been published by our predecessors
on this subject. These are the same flowers which I offer to you,
my reader, but the bouquet which I have made with them will be
different from them, by reason of the difference of the arrangement in which it is put together.'

The distinctive characteristic of the 'bouquet' of Saint Francis
de Sales and his peculiar contribution to the Christian life is that
he envisaged a spirituality for all, not modelled on monastic ob-
servances but framed to meet the needs of the married and those
following ordinary avocations in the world, as he himself said:

'My intention is to instruct those who live in towns, in households, at the court, and who, on account of circumstances, are obliged to lead a common life as far as externals are concerned.' Before going on to examine in greater detail the writings of the saint, something must be said about the circumstances of his own life and work, which eminently fitted him to declare that he wished to show to those who lived amidst the press of temporal affairs that 'just as mother of pearl shells live in the sea, without taking in a drop of sea-water, and that near the Chelidonian islands in the Mediterranean there are springs of fresh water in the middle of the sea, and that night butterflies fly in the flames without burning their wings, so also a strong and faithful soul may live in the world, and, without receiving a single wordly temper, may find the sources of a gentle piety in the midst of the bitter waves of this century, and may fly between the flames of earthly lusts without burning the wings of the sacred desires of the devout life.'

Saint Francis de Sales was born at the Castle of Sales in Savoy in 1567. After studying first at Annecy, then at Paris (1581–8) and at Padua (1588–92) he could have found in the world a brilliant career to which his position, education and eminent capabilities entitled him. An overwhelming sense of vocation to the priesthood, however, caused him to abandon all secular ambitions, and in 1593 he was ordained priest and made Provost of Geneva. His conviction that Christians could follow the way of perfection whatever their state of life did not lead him to minimize either the importance of special vocations or the urgency with which they should be obeyed. Perhaps he was not unmindful of his own response to his vocation when he reminded his hearers in a sermon for the Feast of the Presentation :

'See how the Holy Virgin heard the word of God, and kept it. . . . Our Lord spoke in her ear, or rather in her inmost heart, these words of the psalmist : "Hearken, O daughter, incline thine ears, and forget thy people and thy father's house, and the king shall greatly desire thy beauty." Take notice of these words,

"Hearken, my daughter" as if he wished to say To hear well, it is necessary to listen well; "Incline thine ear" it is necessary to abase and humble ourselves so as to hear well what is the will of God. . . . O holy and blessed invitation, which God often makes in the heart of so many creatures. Nevertheless, it is true that many hear the sacred voice of vocation, yet without leaving their country and without going whither God calls them. They have made so many enquiries and considerations as to whether the inspiration is valid and comes from God and as to whether they should act upon it or not, and they always delay, nevertheless, to go when God calls. I do not say this to discourage legitimate considerations made to determine better the nature of the inspiration. But after so considering, come forth and go into the land which God is showing you; do not listen to so many arguments, nor lend an ear to so many reasons which the world will offer; do not brook any delays or second thoughts, for this you place yourself in great danger. Do not go to sleep but be quick to obey and to follow the leading.'

In the same year as he was ordained Saint Francis de Sales started on a mission to win Chablais from Calvinism to Catholicism. Of the difficulties that attended this task and the zeal with which he carried it out much can be learnt from his extant letters and those of his correspondents. In one letter, dated from Chablais, September 1596, he wrote to Charles Emmanuel, the first Duke of Savoy, informing him as to what was necessary to bring about the establishment, propagation and continuance of the Catholic Faith in Chablais. His provisions even included the suggestion that it would be good to form a troop of police or cavalry, in which the young men would take part, provided that 'this troop were religious and organized according to Christian piety.' Despite the duke's support it was only after great difficulty and much personal suffering that the young priest's efforts were successful. Throughout his ministry he revealed himself as an ardent champion of the Counter-Reformation, often in circumstances which brought him into great danger. So enraged against him on one occasion, in 1603, were the people of Gex that they contrived to poison him. His doctors were quick to recognize the cause of his fever and were able to save his life. It was no purely academic conviction that enabled him to encourage others when they were afflicted with dire physical sufferings with the reflection that suffering provides one with 'the most certain and the most royal road to heaven.' Despite the fact that he lived in an age which knew the bitterness of religious strife, and despite the fact that he had suffered personally at the hands of his Protestant opponents, he acted towards them in a spirit of charity and counselled others to do the same, as for example, when he wrote thus to Mme. de Chantal in 1606 : 'I said that you might see the Huguenots; I say now, Yes, see them, but rarely; and make the encounter brief, nevertheless be gentle with them, and shining in humility and simplicity.'

Four years before writing the letter just quoted, Saint Francis de Sales had been consecrated Bishop of Geneva. During the twenty years of his episcopate he not only shouldered the administration of his diocese, but he was much in demand as preacher, confessor and director of souls. From the letters which he wrote to fellow-bishops one can observe how seriously he regarded the office, both in respect of its administrative and pastoral responsibilities. It is, however, as a chief pastor of the flock committed to his care that his episcopate was so outstanding. His conception of the pastoral office which influenced all his activities is simply and plainly expressed at the end of his preface to the *Introduction to the Devout Life:* 'It is my opinion, my reader, my friend, that being a bishop, God desires me to paint on people's hearts not only the ordinary virtues but that very dear and much loved devotion to God himself. . . . '

Whereas it was the saintly bishop's chief care and delight to lead souls in the paths of true devotion, his concern was not only for those engaged in secular callings or for the conversion of protestants. A great deal of his time was spent in directing Religious and in giving counsel to the heads of Religious Houses.

For none had he a greater affection than for the Visitandine Sisters, whose community he and Mme. de Chantal were instrumental in founding in 1610. The spirit which he hoped would enflame their lives and devotion was that which found expression, for example, in the closing words of a sermon preached before some of the Sisters of the Community on the Feast of the Visitation : 'O my dear Sisters, daughters of the Visitation of our Lady and Saint Elizabeth, who have the Virgin for Mother, how great must be your concern to imitate her, particularly in her humility and charity, the two virtues which especially prompted her to make that holy visit. You ought to shine particularly in those two virtues, showing great diligence and joy in visiting your sick sisters, doing everything possible to comfort and serve one another heartily in your infirmities, whether spiritual or physical, and finally, whenever it is a question of exercising humility and charity, you must do so with outstanding care and diligence. For to be the daughters of our Lady it is not enough to be contented with living in the houses of the Visitation and with wearing the veil of a Religious . . . you must imitate her in her holiness and her virtues. Be, therefore, most careful to model your life upon hers; be gentle, humble, charitable and meek, and continually magnify the Lord with her, and believe, my beloved, that if you do this faithfully and humbly during the course of this mortal life, then when it is over you will sing in heaven with the same Virgin : "Magnificat anima mea Dominum." '

The warm human sympathy with which Saint Francis de Sales helped and encouraged those who came, or wrote, to him for guidance not only inspired in them confidence and encouragement to persevere in the spiritual life but endeared their holy, yet lovable counsellor to them. Indeed, one of the saint's greatest gifts was his facility for making friends, a gift which he consecrated to the full in his care of souls. One cannot read his letters without being deeply moved by the individual care and love which he expended, despite the administrative burdens of his office, on all his spiritual children in his prayer for them and in his dealings with them, not least that he made time to write long letters to them if he felt that by so doing he would serve their spiritual needs. He was, no doubt, writing out of his own experience of the strength of Christian friendship and the happiness of spiritual kinships, such as he enjoyed with Mme. de Chantal and other intimate friends, when he wrote thus in the *Introduction* of genuine legitimate friendship : 'It will be excellent because it comes from God; excellent, because it stretches out towards God; excellent, because its bond is God; excellent, because it will endure eternally in God. Oh! how good it is to love on earth as they love in heaven, and to learn to cherish one another in this world, as we shall do eternally in the other. I am not speaking now about the simple love of charity, for we must have charity towards all men; but I am speaking of spiritual friendship, by which two or three or several friends communicate to one another their devotion, their spiritual affections and thus make themselves of one mind. With what good reason can such happy souls sing "O how good and joyful a thing it is, brethren, to dwell together in unity!" Yea, for the delightful balm of devotion is distilled from one heart to another by constant sharing, so that one can say that God has shed his blessing on that friendship which will last for ever. . . . Perfection, therefore, does not consist in not having any friendships, but in having only those which are good, holy and sacred' (*III, XIX*).

Yet he was aware of the difficulties and dangers involved and his letters and instructions are not lacking in sound, practical advice for the avoidance of foolish friendships amongst people in the world, of unwise friendships between confessors and their penitents, and of particular or exclusive friendships between members of Religious Orders.

It is, moreover, only the mistaken or prejudiced reader who will imagine that there was anything easy-going or sentimental either in the personality of Saint Francis de Sales or in the advice that he gave. One has only to read his two most important works, the *Introduction to the Devout Life* and the *Treatise on the Love of God* to be assured of that. The first part of the former is almost entirely concerned with the necessary discipline required to purge the soul of mortal and venial sins, of sinful affections, and of any inclinations that might prove useless, dangerous or detrimental to the soul's progress. A great part of the essential thesis of the *Treatise on the Love of God* rests on, and expounds, the importance of the will in the spiritual life, for example : 'We are to will our salvation in such sort as God wills it; now he wills it by way of desire, and we also must incessantly desire it, following his desire. Nor does he will it only, but in effect gives us all necessary means to attain it. We then, in fulfilment of the desire we have to be saved, must not only will, but in effect accept all the graces which he has provided for us and offers to us. It is enough to say : I desire to be saved. But with regard to the means of salvation, it is not enough to say : I desire them; but we must, with an absolute resolution, will and embrace the graces which God presents to us; for our will must correspond with God's. And inasmuch as it gives us the means of salvation, we ought to receive them, as we ought to desire salvation in such sort as God desires it for us, and because he desires it.' [1] It has been noted that one of the great contributions which Saint Francis de Sales made to the epoch in which he lived was the part that he played in the Counter-Reformation. Opposed though he was to the theological presuppositions of the Huguenots, and although his devotion had nothing in common with those on the Continent or elsewhere who represented the practise of religion as an austere or gloomy affair, Saint Francis de Sales, nevertheless, had one important characteristic in common with John Calvin, as M. Lanson pointed out.

'Despite all the difference of his temper, Saint Francis de Sales is the continuer of Calvin : he makes theology the subject-matter of literature, because, giving up scholasticism he speaks to every Christian, to every reasoning mind. One only has to be human, to be looking for a rule of life, to understand and to appreciate

[1] Bk. VIII, Ch. IV, Mackey, p. 333.

him. For here, certainly, all the technicalities of theology remain outside.' [2] Later on in the same century the great comedian, Molière, was going to make all France laugh at Tartuffe, the religious hypocrite. Be it noted, however, that Molière was mocking the insincere and the spurious, not the devout and genuine. Indeed, Tartuffe, typical of false devotion, stands out all the more clearly because Saint Francis de Sales a generation earlier had delineated the characteristics of true devotion for people living in the world, and for people of quality in particular.

In his letters and sermons as well as in his *Introduction to the Devout Life* Saint Francis de Sales frequently defined what he understood true devotion to be, how it was exercised, and how it differed from counterfeit forms. The opening chapters of the first book of the *Introduction* describe the nature of true devotion and its application to people of all kinds and of all professions. A very succinct definition of true devotion is to be found in a letter of the saint written in 1604, to Madame Rose Bourgeois, the Abbess of the Royal Abbey of Puits d'Orbe, to whom he wrote many letters of spiritual direction. He says : 'Devotion is none other than the promptness, fervour, affection and activity which one devotes to the service of God, and there is a difference between a good man and a devout man : for he is a good man who keeps the commandments of God, even though he does not do so with great promptness and fervour, but he is a devout man, who not only observes them, he even observes them willingly, promptly and with great courage.'

After a similar passage in another letter written about six months later than the one just quoted, to Madame La Presidente Brulart, he goes on to define 'several rules which it is necessary to observe if one is to be truly devout,' also demonstrating the particular degree to which Saint Francis de Sales brought a life of spiritual perfection within reach of 'all' sorts and conditions of men.' He observes that, 'Before everything else it is necessary to observe the general commandments of God and the Church,

[2] *Histoire de la Littérature française,* p. 342. Tr. mine.

which are established for every faithful Christian; and without that there can be no devotion whatever; every one knows that. Besides the general commandments, it is necessary to observe carefully the particular commandments which each person has regarding his vocation. . . . As for example, bishops are commanded to visit their flock, to teach, to correct and to console them : were I to spend all the week in prayer, were I to fast all my life, and did not do that, I should be lost. Were a person in the married state to work miracles and did not carry out the obligations of a married person, or did not look after her children, she is "worse than an unbeliever," says Saint Paul, and so on with regard to others.'

The second part of the *Introduction* demonstrates how, by the two principal means of the Sacraments and Prayer, the devout soul may be brought into an ever deepening unity with the divine Majesty of God. One of the most lasting and perennially relevant contributions that the *Introduction* makes to those who (like Philothea, the 'lover of God' to whom it was originally addressed) wish to advance in the life of prayer, is the method of meditation which Saint Francis de Sales proposes and expounds in this part of the work. Philothea lives as much in the twentieth century as in the seventeenth, judging by the opening remarks of Book II, chapter II of the *Introduction*. 'But perhaps you do not know, Philothea, how to make mental prayer; for it is something which unfortunately, few people know in our generation; that is why I offer you this simple and brief method. . . .'

The simple and brief method which has been of great help ever since, to multitudes of ordinary Christian folk who want to pray better, may be summarized as follows. The first part of the meditation, the preparation, consisted of two parts, first that of placing oneself in the presence of God, and secondly that of invoking his assistance. The four means which the saint suggests for placing oneself in the Presence of God are to recollect that God is everywhere and therefore where one is; or that God is in one's heart and soul; or that our Saviour in his humanity looks down upon us; or to imagine Christ present with us in his sacred Humanity. It is not suggested that all these four methods of recollecting the Presence of God should be used at once but rather 'one at a time, and then briefly and simply.'

Explaining what he means by 'invocation,' the second part of the preparation, Saint Francis de Sales says :

'Your soul, feeling itself to be in the presence of God, prostrates itself with the utmost reverence, knowing itself to be quite unworthy of remaining in the presence of so sovereign a Majesty; and, nevertheless, knowing that that same goodness desires it, it asks him for grace to serve him and adore him in this meditation.'

After recollecting the Presence of God and invoking his aid, the soul is recommended to make what some authors call the 'reconstruction of place,' and others, an 'interior lesson.' 'For example,' says Saint Francis de Sales, 'if you wish to meditate upon our Saviour on the Cross, you will imagine that you are on Mount Calvary, and that you see everything that is done and said on the day of the Passion; or, if you like, for it is all one, you will imagine that in the very place where you are the Crucifixion of our Saviour takes place, in the manner which the Evangelists describe.'

Then comes the major part of the meditation in which the soul gives itself to considering what lessons it may learn from the subject of meditation. Sometimes it will linger over one 'consideration,' at other times it will pass from one to another like bees amongst the flowers. The soul will then pass from the considerations of the intellect to the stirring of the affections and the resolutions of the will, and these not in general terms but with regard to particular situations, individuals, temptations and so on. From there the soul passes to the conclusion, which should consist of thanksgiving, self-offering, petition and intercession.

To the accumulated wisdom of the spiritual masters of the past Saint Francis de Sales added not only the simplicity, limpidity and forcefulness of his style, but his suggestion that at the end of the meditation one should gather a 'spiritual bouquet' to take with one through the day. By that he meant : 'our spirit having discoursed on some mystery by means of meditation, we must choose one or two points which we shall have found more to our taste and more appropriate to our advancement, for us to remember for the rest of the day and to smell spiritually.'

Saint Francis de Sales was as aware as any of the masters of the spiritual life previously studied in this series that many souls pass beyond the stage of discursive meditation as God bestows upon them varying degrees of contemplative prayer. His great masterpiece on the contemplative life and the union of the soul with God, the *Treatise on the Love of God,* discusses the whole range of the soul's relationship with God. That relationship is essentially and ultimately one that can be expressed in terms of Love, God's love for man and man's response, a response that involves total commitment and the full employment of all the faculties of body, mind and spirit. The dogmatic and moral theologian, the bishop and the humble, penitent child of God, the lover of God faithfully pursuing the way of discursive prayer and the contemplative who has left it behind, all meet in Saint Francis de Sales as he, devout lover of God, sings the praises of divine love :

'O heavenly love, how lovely art thou to our souls!
And blessed be the goodness of God for ever, who so earnestly commands us to love him, though this love is so desirable and so necessary to our happiness that without it we cannot but be miserable.' [3]

True happiness, like true devotion, consists in recognizing and accepting the power of God's love and in living in the light of it. To possess the royalty of inward happiness is, to use again the expression of Saint Francis de Sales, to imbibe 'springs of fresh water in the middle of the sea.' To direct souls in the spiritual life is to lead them to possess even more surely that security in

[3] Bk. X, II, Mackey, p. 413.

God, which is like the house in the Lord's parable that had its foundations upon a rock.

Space does not permit the present author to comment upon all the salient teaching of Saint Francis de Sales but special mention must be made of two characteristic and practical points which are of particular value in helping the individual soul, in all circumstances and at all stages of the spiritual pilgrimage, to retain a sense of security in God. The first is what is known as the doctrine of intention, whereby the soul offers all its powers and activities to be united with the Divine Will and to be used in accordance with God's good pleasure. To abandon oneself wholly to divine Providence is to produce the fruits of peace and humility in the soul. Thus Saint Francis de Sales wrote to one of his spiritual daughters : 'Let us have,' he said, 'a very singleminded intention to desire in all things the honour and glory of God. Let us do the little that we can to that end, following the advice of our spiritual father; and let us leave to God all the rest. Whoever has God as the object of his intentions, and who does what he can, why should he torment himself? Why is he troubled? What has he to fear? No, no, God is not so terrible to those whom he loves, he contents himself with little, for he knows well that we have not much.'

Closely allied to the doctrine of intention is that of 'holy indifference,' a phrase which too easily, perhaps, suggests the wrong connotation of meaning to the twentieth century reader, as it sometimes did in the past to other readers, notably such eminent spiritual writers as Bossuet and Fénelon themselves. But a careful reading of the saint's works, especially the *Treatise on the Love of God* makes his meaning plain. It is, quite simply, the readiness to do the Will of God in all things. 'The indifferent heart,' says Saint Francis de Sales, 'is as a ball of wax in the hands of its God, receiving with equal readiness all the impressions of the Divine pleasure. Therefore whereas God's will is in various things, it chooses, at any cost, that in which it appears most. . . . God's will is found in the service of the poor and of the rich, but yet somewhat more in serving the poor; the indifferent heart will choose that side. God's will lies in moderation amid consolations, and in patience amid tribulations. The indifferent heart prefers the latter, as having more of God's will in it. To conclude, God's will is the sovereign object of the indifferent soul; wheresoever she sees it she runs after the odour of its perfumes, directing her course ever thither where it most appears, without considering anything else. She is conducted by the Divine will, as by a beloved chain; which way ever it goes, she follows it.' [4]

Of the fundamental difference between the passive submission or 'indifference' of the Christian and that of the Moslem, Fr. Northcott has written with penetrating insight in his great book to which frequent reference has already been made : 'The individual Christian's desire must be to know what God means him to do in each case, and then to give himself to that with his whole heart. But his attitude differs entirely from that of the Moslem. The latter also tends to take all that comes as proceeding from the will of God, and his reaction is one of passive submission, but of submission, not to God, but to the event itself. So in the face of sickness or evil he merely lies down under it, as yielding to a greater power. The Christian, on the other hand, looks always straight to God, seeking him and his will in the event. If it is disease he accepts it willingly, yet as an obstacle which God means him to use all his power to overcome. Or, face to face with oppression of the poor, he sees there something allowed by the permissive will of God, but at the same time an opportunity to call forth his courage and love in combatting it. But it makes all the difference to know that he is dealing with a state of affairs that is under the control of God All-Mighty, and not with a world that has broken loose.' [5]

The confines of a single chapter do not permit one to comment on the emphasis which Saint Francis de Sales laid upon, for example, the importance of having a spiritual director, of making

[4] Bk. IX, Ch. IV, Mackey, pp. 374–5.
[5] op. cit., p. 234.

an annual spiritual retreat and of making frequent ejaculatory prayers. Neither is there space to comment fully on the use the saint made of the sermon as a means of deepening the spiritual life of his hearers. Perhaps, at least, sufficient quotation has been made from his sermons to enable us to concur with the judgment of M. Lanson : 'My Lord of Geneva was the true restorer of the eloquence of the pulpit. He had found its true principle, namely, to speak affectionately and devoutly, simply and frankly, and with confidence.' [6] In his own diocese Saint Francis de Sales put into practice the method of preaching which he described in a long letter to the Archbishop of Bourges, Mme. de Chantal's brother, and his own sermons were an exemplification of the advice he gave to one who was about to be raised to the episcopate.

'. . . the first and principal duty of the bishop is to preach. . . . Do not preach in order to become a great preacher, but simply because it is your duty and God wills it : the fatherly sermon of a bishop is of more value than all the artifice of elaborate sermons of preachers of a different kind. For a bishop, very little is needed to preach well; for his sermons must be about necessary and useful things, not matters of enquiry nor research; his words simple and without affectation; his gesture fatherly and natural, unstudied and unrehearsed; and however short the sermon and however little he says, it is always much.'

The spirit of Saint Francis de Sales, the purpose to which he devoted his life and energy, and the lasting influence of his spiritual teaching may be found to be both expressed and summarized in the concluding paragraph of a sermon he once preached for some of his spiritual daughters one Christmas Eve :

'I desire for you, my dear daughters, grace to stand very close to this sacred Saviour, who came to be born here below to gather us all around him, in order that he might keep us always under the standard of his most holy protection, even as we see that the shepherd forms his flock to rule, preserve and govern it, and like the king of the bees who never comes out of the hive except when

[6] op. cit., p. 342.

he is surrounded by his little nation. His goodness will give us the grace to hear his voice and to follow him faithfully, so that, recognizing him for our chief Shepherd in this life we shall not stray, nor listen to the voice of our enemy who hovers around us with the intention of confounding us and devouring us like a hellish wolf; and the grace of faithfulness that we may remain always submissive, obedient and subject to his holy will, so that by this means we begin to do here on earth below what by the help of his grace we shall do eternally in heaven. Amen!'

BIBLIOGRAPHY

SAINT BENEDICT

The Rule of Saint Benedict in Latin and English, ed. Abbot Justin McCann. Burns Oates, 1952.

ABBOT DELATTE, *The Rule of Saint Benedict, Commentary.* Burns Oates, 1921.

DOM DAVID KNOWLES, *The Monastic Order in England.* 1950.

M. DEANESLY, *A History of the Medieval Church.*

L. BOUYER, *La Spiritualité du Nouveau Testament et des Pères.* 1960.

Christian Spirituality To-day, ed. M. Ramsey. Faith Press, 1961.

SAINT BERNARD OF CLAIRVAUX

Saint Bernard of Clairvaux, Vita Prima Bernard. Translated by Geoffrey Webb and Adrian Walker. Mowbrays, 1960.

Cantica Canticorum. Translated and edited by Samuel J. Eales. London, 1895.

The Letters of Saint Bernard of Clairvaux. Translated and edited by Bruno Scott James. B.O.W., 1953.

On the Love of God. Translated by a Religious of the C.S.M.V. Mowbrays, 1950.

H. DANIEL-ROPS, *Cathedral and Crusade: Studies of the Medieval Church.* Tr. Warrington. J. M. Dent, 1957.

Quand un saint arbitrait l'Europe. Fayard, 1953.

KNOWLES, *The Monastic Order in England,* 1950.

DOM CUTHBERT BUTLER, *Western Mysticism.* Constable, 1922. (Also available as a paper-back.)

ETIENNE GILSON, *The Mystical Theology of Saint Bernard.* Sheed and Ward, 1940.

SAINT FRANCIS OF ASSISI

THOMAS DE CELANO, *The First and Second Lives of Saint Francis.* Tr. A. G. Ferrers Howell.

SAINT BONAVENTURA, *Legenda Sancti Francisci.*

The Legend of the Three Companions. Temple Classics.

The Mirror of Perfection. Temple Classics.

The Little Flowers of Saint Francis. Penguin Books.

FR. CUTHBERT, O.S.F.C., *The Life of Saint Francis.* Longmans.

J. R. H. MOORMAN, *Sources for the Life of Saint Francis.*
  Saint Francis of Assisi.

SAINT FRANCIS, *Works.* London, 1882.

LEO SHERLEY-PRICE, *Lent with Saint Francis.*

FR. STANISLAS MAJARELLI, O.F.M., *Assisi.*

L. VON MATT, *Saint Francis of Assisi.* A pictorial biography.

La Spiritualité du Moyen Age, ed. Bouyer, Vandenbroucke and
    Leclercq.

M. D. LAMBERT, *Franciscan Poverty.*

E. GOUDGE, *Saint Francis of Assisi.*

RAMON LULL

E. A. PEERS, *Ramon Lull, a Biography.* S.P.C.K., 1929.
  Fool of Love. S.C.M., 1945.
  Studies of the Spanish Mystics, 2 vols.

RAMON LULL, *The Book of the Lover and the Beloved.* Tr. Peers.
    S.P.C.K., 1946.
  Blanquerna. Tr. Peers. London, 1926.

JAN VAN RUYSBROECK

JAN VAN RUYSBROECK, *The Adornment of the Spiritual Marriage.*
  The Sparkling Stone.
    The Book of Supreme Truth. Tr. C. A. W. Dom, ed. E. Under-
      hill, 1916.
    The Seven Steps of the Ladder of Spiritual Love. Tr. F. Sher-
      wood Taylor. 1952 ed.

H. NORTHCOTT, C.R., *The Venture of Prayer.* S.P.C.K., 1950.

La Spiritualité du Moyen Age. L. Bouyer and others. Aubier,
    1960.

BIBLIOGRAPHY

SAINT TERESA OF AVILA

The Complete Works of Saint Teresa, ed. E. A. Peers. Volumes I, II, and III. Sheed and Ward.

E. A. PEERS, 2 Vols. *Studies of the Spanish Mystics.* 1927–30.
Way Up. C.L.A., 1951.
The Mystics of Spain. Allen and Unwin. 1951.
Saint Teresa of Jesus and other Essays and Addresses. Faber and Faber, 1953.

E. L. MASCALL, *A Guide to Mount Carmel.* Dacre Press, 1939.

SAINT JOHN OF THE CROSS

Saint John of the Cross, Complete Works, ed. E. A. Peers. B.O.W.

E. A. PEERS, *Spirit of Flame.* S.C.M. 1961 ed.

GABRIEL OF SAINT MARY MAGDALENE, *Saint John of the Cross, Doctor of Divine Love and Contemplation.* 1946.

SAINT FRANCIS DE SALES

Introduction à la Vie Dévote. Paris, 1932.
Lettres. Paris, 1821.
Sermons. Paris, 1821.
Treatise on the Love of God. Tr. H. B. Mackey. B.O.W., 1884.
E. K. SANDERS, *Life of Saint Francis de Sales.* 1928.

(Translations mine.)